Trans

The Cathedral Builders

Evergreen Profile Book 21

GROVE PRESS, INC.   EVERGREEN BOOKS LTD.
NEW YORK   LONDON

FIRST PUBLISHED IN THIS EDITION 1961. ALL RIGHTS RESERVED.

Library of Congress Catalog Card Number: 60-6216

Evergreen Profile Books are published
in the United States by Grove Press, Inc.
64 University Place   New York 3, N.Y.
in Great Britain by Evergreen Books Ltd.
20 New Bond Street   London, W. 1

First published in France by Éditions du Seuil, Paris, as Les Batisseurs de Cathédrales

MANUFACTURED BY MOUTON & CO., IN THE NETHERLANDS

The Cathedral Builders
by Jean Gimpel

Contents

THE FANTASTIC MIDDLE AGES

In a period of three centuries, from 1050 to 1350, several million tons of stone were quarried in France to build eighty cathedrals, five hundred large churches, and tens of thousands of parish churches. More stone was quarried in France during these three centuries than in ancient Egypt during its whole history – and the Great Pyramid alone has a volume of 40,500,000 cubic feet. Foundations of some of the great cathedrals were imbedded as deep as thirty feet – the average depth of a Paris subway station – and in certain cases formed a stone mass as large as that above ground.

In the Middle Ages there was one church or chapel for approximately every two hundred people. These cult edifices consequently covered a considerable area in ratio to the small cities of the time. For example, in Norwich, Lincoln, and York – cities of five to ten thousand inhabitants – there were, respectively, fifty, forty-nine, and forty-one churches. The ambitious who wanted to reconstruct their church on a larger plot were always faced with serious problems: it was often necessary to destroy one or two neighboring churches and build new lodgings for the expropriated. The area of Amiens Cathedral, covering about 208,000 square feet, permitted the entire population of nearly ten thousand people to attend the same service. For comparison, imagine in a modern city of one million people a stadium built in the middle of town large enough to accommodate the whole population, remembering that the largest stadium in the world seats only 180,000.

5

Nave, tower, and spire heights are astonishing. An architect could build a fourteen-story building in the choir of Beauvais Cathedral before reaching the vault, 157 feet 6 inches above the floor. To equal the masters of Chartres, who pushed their cathedral's spire up to 345 feet 6 inches, the present municipality would have to build a thirty-story skyscraper. To equal the Strasbourgers who raised their spire to 466 feet would require a forty-story skyscraper.

There is no lack of documentation concerning the builders of these immense edifices; yet there are few situations in which legend is not mixed with historical truth: legends about corporations, secrets, volunteer labor, builder monks, etc.

For half a century French historians and archaeologists, with one worthy exception, have abandoned the study of history and construction to concentrate on interesting questions, but their interests have been so specialized that the complex of problems posed by medieval architecture seems to have escaped them. It was different in the nineteenth century and the beginning of the twentieth, when the French historians considered the subject in its totality. Such names come to mind as Jules Quicherat and Victor Mortet, but above all, Viollet-le-Duc, whom it is now fashionable to criticize. Yet one need only reread his *Discourses on Architecture* and his *Dictionnaire raisonné de l'Architecture française du XIe au XVIe Siècle* to realize that he was one of the great men of the nineteenth century. He made mistakes, surely, but who doesn't? His knowledge of medieval society and the history of construction is remarkable even today. He is reproached for having reconstructed the Château de Pierrefonds with a certain "brutality," which is true, but the ruinous state of the château, which Napoleon III demanded be restored, must not be forgotten. If Viollet-le-Duc had not worked energetically, many of the buildings we admire today would no longer exist. We reproach Viollet-le-Duc his excesses, but we must ask ourselves if the next century will not reproach our restorers of historic monuments for not having spent enough

Château de Pierrefonds: before and after Viollet-le-Duc's restoration

money on laboratory research to discover the cause of stone decay.

But, as mentioned above, one very worthy historian has been an exception. What is more, he is not a medievalist. In 1953 Pierre du Colombier published a remarkable work, *Les Chantiers des Cathédrales,* which is as interesting for the general public as for the specialists to whom it gives numerous references. And whereas French researches have been little inclined to this field until now, English and German scholars have continued the work of the nineteenth century. The latter have primarily studied fourteenth- and fifteenth-century German construction – the period of the great German architectural workshops – but their conclusions must be used judiciously in understanding twelfth- and thirteenth-century workshops because there was, in the second half of the thirteenth century, a transformation of working conditions in Europe, particularly in France.

By contrast, the works undertaken in England during the last thirty years by G. G. Coulton, John Harvey, L. F. Salzman, and especially D. Knoop and G. P. Jones in *The Medieval Mason* and in the periodical *Ars Quatuor Coronatorum* offer a better understanding of workshop life during the "cathedral crusade," and permit scholars to dispel legends that cloud the truth. These historians have recognized the importance of freedom in their work. They have studied with equal precision the evolution of freemasonry transactions and the specific roles of monks in the construction of their abbeys. Unfortunately, their works are little known in Europe and have never been translated. It is one of the paradoxes of the twentieth century that although political news is immediately translated and transmitted throughout the world, and scientific works circulate rapidly, the results of historical research must still wait several decades to cross frontiers. In defense of historians it must be admitted that in this case it is sometimes difficult, not to say impossible, to obtain certain English works. For example, the periodical *Ars Quatuor Coronatorum,* containing works of primary importance, is published in London by Masonic Lodge 2076. This periodical is not sold and therefore is not found in any public library, which is unfortunate, for the lodge has

8

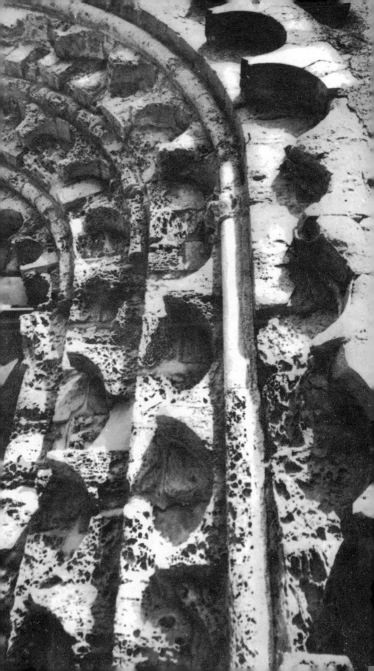

carefully and methodically studied various aspects of medieval construction and, more important, has published the accounts (or pay ledgers) of thirteenth- and fourteenth-century English religious and civil workshops.

All histories of medieval architecture make the classic distinction between Romanesque and Gothic monuments and agree that the transition took place in the mid-twelfth century. This distinction supposes that the Gothic style had specific features such as the flying buttress or the ogival (rib) vault; but many Gothic churches were built

Saint-Germain at Auxerre: a "Romanesque" church (the crypt)

without flying buttresses, and people are finally beginning to realize that the celebrated ogival vaults did not have the importance formerly attributed to them. There was no fundamental distinction between a Romanesque and a Gothic building, but there was an enormous difference between a church of the mid-eleventh century and one of the thirteenth century. This difference was the accumulated result of hundreds of little technical discoveries by ingenious architects and workers – the cathedral builders.

Saint-Étienne at Beauvais: a "Gothic" church

There were no builders of "Romanesque" cathedrals or "Gothic" cathedrals per se, no more than there were Romanesque or Gothic workshops. There were only some builders who created and others who copied them, relying on older techniques. This is important to emphasize. It is amazing to realize that for 250 years, from the end of the thirteenth century to the beginning of the sixteenth, a period during which the transepts of Sens, Senlis, and Beauvais were built, there was practically no progress made in construction technique. Flamboyant Gothic, [1] appearing in the late fourteenth century, was only a superficial decoration added into a technical skeleton perfected from the eleventh through the thirteenth century. For 250 years architects were inventive, and during the following 250 years they were content to copy their predecessors. This halt in architectural development at the end of the thirteenth century was a phenomenon connected to all aspects of medieval history: religious, technical, economic, social, and psychological. The arbitrary separation of Romanesque and Gothic in the middle of the twelfth century corresponds to no particular historical event, whereas the second half of the thirteenth was a striking epoch in the history of the Middle Ages. The period from 1050 to the second half of the thirteenth century was, for Europe in general and France in particular, a dynamic period of ascendancy. It was an age of creativity during the course of which some of the greatest spirits of the Western world were to pray, teach, or govern – St. Bernard, Abélard, St. Francis of Assisi, St. Thomas Aquinas, Roger Bacon, or St. Louis. And the cathedral builders were to raise those extraordinary churches that would be testimonals of this high epoch of medieval Christianity.

If a date must be chosen to mark the end of the dynamic spiritual enthusiasm of this society, it would be 1277, the year of the doctrinal condemnations by the Bishop of Paris and the date when Thomism became confused with Averronism. Gabriel Le Bras writes on this subject, "During half a century, from 1227 to 1277, canon law reached the height of its course," and adds,

the decline of medieval Christianity announces itself

Notre-Dame de l'Epine near Châlons-sur-Marne

in the new spiritual state and feeling with which canon law tried to exorcise the revolt against the established Church, the affirmation of the independence of civil societies, and the development of the plastic arts and sacred music.

We will return to this general crisis, after which the Western world entered definitively into its modern age, long before that period we conveniently call the "Renaissance."

13

ST. BERNARD AND ABBOT SUGER

The spread of Christianity and the history of medieval builders are closely connected with the development of monasticism. In the sixth century St. Benedict founded Monte Cassino and formulated his Rule of Life. It spread with amazing speed from one place to another and Europe was soon covered with Benedictine monasteries. Benedict's Rule must be considered one of the great historical events of the Middle Ages. It organized the spiritual life, arranging manual labor around the seven Canonical Hours. This gave it its force, yet its observance became relaxed at certain times, necessitating a reform of the Benedictine order. Two such reforms are especially interesting: that of Cluny in the tenth century and that of Cîteaux in the twelfth. The Cluniac reform followed the Saracen, Norman, and Magyar raids that ended the Carolingian Renaissance and threw the Benedictines into a life of confusion and laxity. At the beginning of the tenth century, William the Pious, Duke of Aquitaine, founded at the small village of Cluny the monastery from which the prodigious Cluniac spirit was diffused. Its civilizing influence on the Western world must have been preponderant. In several years, in a feudal and brutal world, Cluniac monks covered Europe from Poland to Portugal with some fourteen hundred houses and dependencies.

To keep in touch with his abbots and priors, the Abbot-Father of Cluny periodically called assemblies to which representatives of the monasteries came to report on the state of each community and receive instructions. The

15

Abbot of Cluny worked ceaselessly to enlarge his monastery to accomodate the hundreds of delegates who came from every part of France, Spain, and Hungary. By the beginning of the twelfth century the abbey could lodge 460 monks and handle two thousand visitors. The immense church constructed between 1080 and 1135, and destroyed under the Empire, was as large as St. Peter's in Rome.

The problems posed in constructing these fourteen hundred Cluniac monasteries brought about a considerable advance in the science of construction in western Europe. The first abbeys were built of wood since the art of stonecutting had all but been lost. St. Odilon, Abbot of Cluny, made this explicit when he said, "I found a wooden abbey and left it in marble." He had antique marble columns shipped to Cluny via the Danube and Rhône rivers. In organizing the pilgrimage to Santiago de Compostela to induce pilgrims into Spain and interest Europe in the Christian reconquest of Moorish-occupied Spain, Cluny encouraged the construction or enlargement of vast basilicas on this important pilgrimage route.

The Cluniac order gave a number of popes to the papacy, among them, Gregory VII, the great eleventh-century Pope, and Urban II, who preached the First Crusade in 1096. The order was headed by such men as St. Hugues, one of the most perfect representatives of the monastic ideal, and Peter the Venerable, the last great abbot of Cluny, who had the genius to have the Koran translated with geographical and historical references to the beliefs of Islam in order to fight the Moslem world on an intellectual level.

At the end of the eleventh century the Cluniacs relaxed from a strict observance of St. Benedict's Rule. And in 1098, St. Robert, Abbot of Molesmes, founded a monastery in the middle of the swampy forest at Cîteaux (Diocese of Langres) to reform the Rule. This new monastery really began to prosper only in 1112 when Bernard, a young nobleman of the region, entered it with a few companions. When Bernard died in 1153, the Cistercian order had 343 monasteries and before the end of the century, 530. St. Bernard, *the* spirit and power of the order, organized the Second Crusade in 1147 and was

Urban II dedicating Cluny

the arbiter of European politics as well as Christianity's chief officer. His determination to comply with absolute strictness to St. Benedict's Rule had important spiritual, social, economic, and technical consequences.

Cluny's success was due to the desire of pious and energetic men hoping to pull Christian Europe out of the barbarism of the tenth and eleventh centuries. Cîteaux's success was due to the austere will of a group desiring to retire from the vain pleasures of the Western world in which a *joie de vivre* and a materialistic spirit were beginning to spread. The West, having lived in economic

17

isolation since the collapse of the Roman Empire, began to sense its own material destitution on contact with the Orient and the commercial activities in Italian cities during the First Crusade. Society coveted precious stones, ivory, perfume, and beautiful silks from the Orient.

St. Bernard and his companions withdrew from the world in which this taste for life and luxury, even among the Cluniacs, had replaced the love of God. To protect them from every worldly temptation, the order required its monks to rid themselves of every luxury and retire to the forests. Having cleared the woods and created model farms of several hundred acres – in contrast to the great artisan, feudal farms – the Cistercians built their great abbeys. The order's constructions reflected the austerity of its Rule. Neither towers nor porches were built; there was no sculpture and no stained glass windows. Whereas Cluniac churches were covered with gold and paintings, Cistercian churches were bare. Stones were left undressed.

In his famous letter addressed to the Cluniacs, St. Bernard lashed out at the rich color of their churches:

> I say naught of the vast height of your [Cluniac] churches, their immoderate length, their superfluous breadth, the costly polishings, the curious carvings and paintings which attract the worshipper's gaze and hinder his attention, and seem to me in some sort a revival of the ancient Jewish rites. Let this pass, however: say that this is done for God's honour. But I, as a monk, ask of my brother monks . . . "Tell me, ye poor (if, indeed, ye be poor), what doeth this gold in your sancturay?" And indeed the bishops have an excuse which monks have not; for we know that they, being debtors to the wise and the unwise, and unable to excite the devotion of carnal folk by spiritual things, do so by bodily adornments. But we [monks] who have now come forth from the people; we who have left all the precious and beautiful things of the world for Christ's sake; who have counted but dung, that we may win Christ, all things fair to see or soothing to hear, sweet to smell, delightful to taste, or pleasant to touch – in a word, all bodily delights – whose devotion, pray, do we

18

Aint bernard fu

monks intend to excite by these things? What profit, I say, do we expect therefrom? The admiration of fools, or the oblations of the simple? Or, since we are scattered among the nations, have we perchance learnt their works and do we yet serve their graven images? To speak plainly, doth the root of all this lie in covetousness, which is idolatry; and do we seek not [spiritual] profit, but a gift? If thou askest: "How?" I answer, "In a strange fashion." For money is thus artfully scattered in order that it may multiply; it is expended that it may give increase, and the prodigality giveth birth to plenty; for at the very sight of these costly yet marvellous vanities men are more kindled to offer gifts than to pray. Thus wealth is drawn up by ropes of wealth, thus money bringeth money; for I know not how it is that, wheresoever more abundant wealth is seen, there do men offer more freely. There eyes are feasted with relics cased in gold, and their purse-strings are loosed. They are shown a most comely image of some saint, whom they think all the more saintly that he is the more gaudily painted. Men run to kiss him, and are invited to give; there is more admiration for his comeliness than veneration for his sanctity. . . . The church is resplendent in her walls, beggarly in her poor; she clothes her stones in gold, and leaves her sons naked. . . . *

But St. Bernard's polemics had only a limited influence on Cluniac laxity and, at his death, the General Chapters, the governing body of the order, had to remind certain abbots of the statutes concerning the decoration of their monasteries. Yet St. Bernard's personality was such – and his moral status so high in the Christian world – that during his lifetime nothing was done without his approval. It was for this reason that the great builder, Abbot Suger, regent of France while Louis VII was on the crusade, was forced to write two books justifying his love of splendor, which was manifested in the Benedictine Abbey of Saint-Denis. These books reveal some of the sentiments that

* English tranlation from G. G. Coulton, *Art and the Reformation*, Part II, *The Fate of Medieval Art in the Renaissance and Reformation*, New York, Harper & Bros., 1958, Appendix 26, iv-vi

Saint Bernard (beginning of the fifteenth century)

impelled the men of this age to consecrate an important part of their activity to construction.

In contrast to the majority of the great men of his day, Suger was of humble origin, a fact he never bothered to conceal. Indeed, he was quite probably of peasant stock. At the age of eleven he was admitted to the school of Saint-Denis-de-l'Estrée, in the shadow of the abbey, where he was raised with sons of the French nobility and royal princes. It was there that he began his friendship with the future king of France. He tells us that from his youth his great ambition was to rebuild the abbey: "I completed this [rebuilding of the abbey, save for the nave] all the more gladly because I had wished to do it, if ever I should have an opportunity, even while I was a pupil in school."

For several centuries Saint-Denis had been the royal abbey in which the kings of France were buried. Piously collected, there were the relics of St. Denis and his two legendary companions, St. Rustique and St. Éleuthère, whom Suger called his "Holy Martyrs." Several times, sent on missions to Rome, Suger helped strengthen the oft-broken bonds between the papacy and the king of France. He was there in 1121 when he learned of his appointment as abbot of Saint-Denis. Upon his return to France, he immediately began to lead an ostentatious life. St. Bernard, ever concerned for the dignity of the Church, strongly criticized the new abbot's attitude, and Suger accepted these remonstrances by the Clairvaux abbot, curtailed his way of living, and undertook to reform the abbey, which had a rather attenuated austerity.

In 1127 Bernard sent an amazing letter to Suger in which, after having congratulated him on correcting his way of life, he expressed his desire to have royal favor denied to Étienne de Garlanda, a monk who had been named seneschal. By the end of that year Étienne had been removed from power and for the first time Bernard found himself in direct accord with the king. From that moment on, despite their different temperaments, Bernard and Suger were in agreement. Each realized that his interests did not conflict with the other's: one was the official representative of the papacy, the other the most important political personality in France.

None the less, Suger's boundless passion for richness and splendor probably did more to popularize the taste for luxury and decoration in the Church's services than Cluny ever did. To prevent another attack by St. Bernard, he wrote:

Let every man abound in his own sense. To me, I confess, one thing has always seemed pre-eminently fitting: that every costlier or costliest thing should serve, first and foremost, for the administration of the Holy Eucharist. *If* golden pouring vessels, golden vials, golden little mortars used to serve, by the word of God or the command of the Prophet, to collect the *blood of goats or calves or the red heifer:* how much more must golden vessels, precious stones, and whatever is most valued among all created things, be laid out, with continual reverence and full devotion, for the reception of the *blood of Christ!* Surely neither we nor our possessions suffice for this service. If, by a new creation, our substance were re-formed from that of the holy Cherubim and Seraphim, it would still offer an insufficient and unworthy service for so great and so ineffable a victim; and yet we have so great a propitiation for our sins. The detractors also object that a saintly mind, a pure heart, a faithful intention ought to suffice for this sacred function; and we, too, explicitly and especially affirm that it is these that principally matter. [But] we profess that we must do homage also through the outward ornaments of sacred vessels, and to nothing in the world in an equal degree as to the service of the Holy Sacrifice, with all inner purity and with all outward splendor. *

Suger covered the main altar with gold:

We had it all encased, putting up golden panels on either side and adding a fourth, even more precious one; so that the whole altar would appear golden all the way round.

* English translations of Suger's account from Erwin Panofsky, *Abbot Suger on the Abbey Church of St.-Denis and Its Art Treasures*, Princeton, Princeton University Press, 1946.

23

The "Holy Martyrs," as well as Suger, liked brightness and splendor. Although he had proposed to set up a modest altar before the tomb of St. Denis and his companions, the saints themselves demanded what he should do:

> While we, overcome by timidity, had planned to set up in front of this [altar] a panel golden but modest, the Holy Martyrs themselves handed to us such a wealth of gold and most precious gems – unexpected and hardly to be found among kings – as though they were telling us with their own lips: "Whether thou wantst it or not, we want of it the best."

Thus encouraged, Suger no longer hesitated. He abandoned himself to the joy of acquiring the most beautiful objects. He described the masterpieces he put on the main altar, some of which are now preserved in the Louvre:

> And further we adapted for the service of the altar, with the aid of gold and silver material, a porphyry vase, made admirable by the hand of the sculptor and polisher, after it had lain idly in a chest for many years, converting it from a flagon into the shape of an eagle. We also procured for the services at the aforesaid altar a precious chalice out of one solid sardonyx. . . . Further we added another vase shaped like a ewer, very similar to the former in material but not in form. . . . Still another vase, looking like a pint bottle of beryl or crystal. . . .

Thanks to this intervention by God, the monks brought him the precious stones he needed to ornament the great cross, twenty-one feet high – a true monument of theological science – that he placed in the choir. It was visible from every part of the church.

> One merry but notable miracle which the Lord granted us in this connection [setting up the great crucifix] we do not wish to pass over in silence. For when I was in difficulty for want of gems and could

25

not sufficiently provide myself with more (for their scarcity makes them very expensive): then, lo and behold, [monks] from three abbeys of two Orders – that is, from Cîteaux and another abbey of the same Order, and from Fontevráult – entered our little chamber adjacent to the church and offered us for sale an abundance of gems such as we had not hoped to find in ten years, hyacinths, sapphires, rubies, emeralds topazes. Their owners had obtained them from Count Thibaut for alms; and he in turn had received them, through the hands of his brother Stephen, King of England, from the treasures of his uncle, the late King Henry, who had amassed them throughout his life in wonderful vessels. We, however, freed from the worry of searching for gems, thanked God and gave four hundred pounds for the lot though they were worth much more.

We applied to the perfection of so sacred an ornament not only these but also a great and expensive supply of other gems and large pearls. We remember, if memory serves, to have put in about eighty marks of refined gold. And barely within two years were we able to have completed, through several goldsmiths from Lorraine – at times five, at other times seven – the pedestal adorned with the Four Evangelists; and the pillar upon which the sacred image stands, enameled with exquisite workmanship, and [on it] the history of the Saviour, with the testimonies of the allegories from the Old Testament indicated, and the capital above looking up, with its images, to the Death of the Lord.

In order that these sacred objects be admired and venerated by the faithful, the church choir had to be adequately lighted. So Suger pulled down the somber Carolingian basilica and raised a choir pierced with large windows surrounding the relics, altars, and the great crucifix. Satisfied with the happy effect thus obtained, he wrote an inscription on the glory of light and had it engraved in the church:

> Once the new apse is joined to the old façade
> The center of the sanctuary gleams in its splendor.

Saint-Denis, window: Suger at the feet of the Virgin

What has been splendidly united shines in splendor
And the magnificent work, inundated with a new
[light, shines,
It is I, Suger, who in my day enlarged this edifice,
Under my direction was it done.

The builders of Saint-Denis, like those who had worked
for the Cluniacs, continued to submit to the need for light
just mentioned in connection with Suger. This history of
construction is closely linked with architects' unceasing
efforts to allow openings in the walls without compro-
mising the solidity of their buildings. The many attempts
to make naves and choirs light were more or less success-
ful, although some of the more audacious edifices collapsed. [2] Architects of antiquity, of Islam, or Byzantium

were preoccupied with shielding their interiors from the strong rays of the sun. Rarely before the twelfth century had architects had to build such large buildings in regions as far north as Burgundy and the Île-de-France.

Incentives in addition to those mentioned above inspired Suger's ardent and enthusiastic reconstruction of his abbey. If light were necessary to glorify God properly, it was equally necessary that on feast days the greatest possible number of the faithful be able to approach the holy relics humbly, without crowding. The choir had to be spacious enough to permit an orderly procession of the crowds of believers. To prove the pressing need for a larger choir, Suger vividly described the uproar on a feast day in the old basilica:

> Often on feast days, completely filled, it [the Carolingian basilica] disgorged through all its doors the excess of the crowds as they moved in opposite directions, and the outward pressure of the foremost ones not only prevented those attempting to enter from entering but also expelled those who had already entered. At times you could see, a marvel to behold, that the crowded multitude offered so much resistance to those who strove to flock in to worship and kiss the holy relics, the Nail and Crown of the Lord, that no one among the countless thousands of people because of their very density could move a foot; that no one, because of their very congestion, could [do] anything but stand like a marble statue, stay benumbed or, as a last resort, scream. This distress of the women, however, was so great and so intolerable that [you could see] how they, squeezed in by the mass of strong men as in a winepress, exhibited bloodless faces as in imagined death; how they cried out horribly as though in labor; how several of them, miserably trodden underfoot [but then], lifted by the pious assistance of men above the heads of the crowd, marched forward as though clinging to a pavement; and how many others, gasping with their last breath, panted in the cloister of the brethren to the dispair of everyone. Moreover the brethren who were showing the tokens of the Passion of Our Lord to the visitors had to yield to their anger

28

and rioting and many a time, having no place to turn, escaped with the relics through the windows.

It was important to place altars around the choir so all the priests could celebrate the Mass. To meet this requirement, Suger conceived a plan of radiating chapels that was adopted in numerous churches during the second half of the century.

Suger greatly strengthened the prestige of the king over his vassals by making the royal church the most glorious in France. He thanked God for having reserved for him the honor of rebuilding Saint-Denis. His pride of authorship played no small role in his reconstruction of the abbey, and he provided funds for a feast in his memory in the church, an honor previously accorded only to kings. Wishing to be remembered, he employed means that may occasionally make us smile, but which were by no means ineffective since he and his works are still well known. He had himself represented four times in the abbey, and he wrote thirteen inscriptions in his own honor and had them engraved in stone or metal in various parts of the church. He can be seen at the foot of Christ in Majesty on the tympanum and at the foot of the Virgin in one of the ambulatory windows where his name is inscribed on the glass in letters as tall as those honoring the Mother of God. On the façade of Saint-Denis the inscription that recalls Suger's role in and the date of the consecration of the narthex can still be read:

> For the splendor of the church that has fostered and
> [exalted him,
> Suger has labored for the splendor of the church.
> Giving thee a share of what is thine, O Martyr Denis,
> He prays to thee to pray that he may obtain a share
> [of Paradise.
> The year was the One Thousand, One Hundred,
> [and Fortieth
> Year of the Word when [this structure] was con-
> [secrated.

On a ewer now preserved in the Louvre, he had this verse inscribed: "Since we must offer libations to God with gems and gold, I, Suger, offer this vase to the Lord."

And on the *Justa,* an Egyptian work of the fourth century: "As a bride, Eleanor gave this vase to King Louis, Mitadolus to her grandfather, the king to me, and Suger to the Saints."

Suger's triumph as a "builder" came on the second Sunday in June, 1144, when the choir was consecrated. This day, for which he had prepared with all his genius for organization, perhaps had a greater effect on architecture than any other single day in history. To consecrate the twenty altars at this grandiose ceremony, he assembled the king, all the peers of the realm, archbishops and bishops – among others, those of Sens, Senlis, Soissons, Chartres, Reims, and Beauvais. Impressed by this new abbey, each returned to his cathedral anxious to match this extraordinary spiritual realization.

Since then the centuries have made Saint-Denis so drab that if Suger returned he would doubtless suppose that his abbey had become Cistercian. He would be sure that St. Bernard's austerity had triumphed. The gold-covered altars, the great crucifix, bedecked with jewels, the chalices, and all the treasures have disappeared. The walls have been whitewashed or left bare by recent restorations. The paintings and sculpture have been removed. The choir stalls, pavement, and multicolored tapestries have vanished. More often than not, the brilliant color of Suger is for France only a memory. Cathedrals and Cluniac abbeys which were conceived and built in a spirit very similar to that of Cluny and Saint-Denis are unrecognizable. No longer can the dual qualities of the Christian world, symbolized by St. Bernard on the one hand and by Suger on the other, be compared – only the spirit of Cîteaux remains. Cistercian monasteries remain austere, still secluded from the world. Wall stones are always unpainted, windows clear, and there is never porch, tower, or sculpture.

Why can the medieval concept symbolized by Suger no longer be found in cathedrals and Cluniac abbeys? What spiritual disasters and physical events combined to hide a whole facet of the ascending spirit of Christianity? Is was evidently not a triumph for St. Bernard's austerity. The introduction of Roman law into northern Europe at the end of the thirteenth century led medieval society to the Renaissance and modern times. This Renaissance was the rebirth of the ideas of the ancients, and the cult of antiquity had a catastrophic effect on medieval monuments. When churches were not actually systematically destroyed to be rebuilt according to classical concepts, as for example the Pantheon in Paris, it was only because frequently the considerable expenses necessary prohibited such projects. Churches were transformed little by little to conform to the taste of the time. The widespread destruction during the French Revolution of 1789 was negligible compared to the barbarous depredations of the seventeenth and, particularly, eighteenth centuries. A list of the ravages of the eighteenth century would fill several volumes. And it is incredible that guides persist in enumerating the destructions of the Revolution without mentioning those of the eighteenth century.

Eighteenth-century Christians simply could not believe that medieval works permitted a dignified glorification of God. For them, only their taste and their objects were really worthy of playing this sacred role. And so, in the name of taste, everyone assisted in a formidable game of destruction. The eighteenth century believed itself to possess the *grand goût*; the medieval *petit goût*, or Gothic taste, as it was then derisively called, merited only the sledgehammer and ax of demolition.

At Saint-Denis, to enlarge the entrance to the church and to facilitate the entry and departure of the royal dais when important services took place, the trumeau of the central portal was removed and the statue of St. Denis destroyed. At the same time the lintels of the three portals and the statue-column representing kings and queens of the Old Testament which decorated the jambs were destroyed. There was no hesitancy in ripping up the time-honored stone tombs and the glazed tile floor in the choir to replace them with a black and white pavement. Prior Dom Malaret, responsible for these misdeeds, had no intention of stopping while everything was going so well. He proposed to crowd the royal tombs, then located in the side aisles, into two chapels in the crypt because he found them cumbersome and hideous. From 1781 to 1784, Dom Malaret hired the Italian contractor Borani to whitewash the entire interior of the church.

32

Borani had previously very conscientiously executed this work at Angers, Chartres and Tours.

At Notre-Dame de Paris in 1699, Mansart, famous architect of the Place Vendôme and the dome of the Invalides, destroyed the thirteenth-century high altar, choir screen, stalls, and bas-reliefs which set off the choir enclosure from the apse to set up a new high altar. Medieval stone and copper tombs suffered the same fate. Hemicycle columns disappeared under marble plaques covered with gilt metal ornaments. Some years later workers were recruited to knock out the thirteenth-century stained glass windows to permit more light to enter the interior. In 1752 the great thirteenth-century ambulatory windows shattered under hammer blows, to be replaced by clear glass ornamented with a border of fleur-de-lys.

In 1771 Soufflet, architect of the Pantheon, in order to permit the royal dais to pass under the cathedral porch, broke the Beau-Dieu which had stood majestically on the central portal trumeau. He also removed the sculptures of the wise and foolish virgins placed on each side of the portal as well as those from the tympanum representing the resurrection and St. Michael weighing souls. All these pieces have now been recut, but because of the mortar joints, the original parts of the tympanum are clearly distinguishable from the restoration. As in Saint-Denis and many other churches of the period, the interior of Notre-Dame was whitewashed.

When Louis-André de Grimaldi, a Monacan prince and Bishop of Mans, quit that bishopric in 1777 to go to Noyon, the Mans chapter – in recognition of the "embellishments" he had brought to their cathedral – placed the prelate's portrait in the vestry with a eulogistic inscription on a marble plaque dated 1778. Under his episcopate the thirteenth-century high altar, "a confused heap of stones and copper ornaments," and all the nave, transept, and side-aisle altars disappeared. With the remains of the choir screen two altars were built in the eighteenth-century style. The eight large hemicycle piers disappeared under marble and stucco. Eighteen to twenty thousand pounds of copper were sold. A contemporary antiquarian, Chappotin de Saint-Laurent, tried in vain to prevent the chapter from going through with this act of vandalism; he could not even get permission to copy the old inscriptions engraved on these objects. Thus this immense treasure of the goldsmith's art was lost forever.

Thirteenth-century high altars were replaced by those in the new style. Many of them are still in the choirs (Paris and Chartres). Choir screens were replaced by wrought-iron grills; new chalices, monstrances, and crosses replaced those of the Middle Ages.

The extraordinary thing about these events is that those who perpetrated them were unquestionably inspired by profound religious sentiment. Bishops, canons, and laymen sacrificed much of their personal wealth and well-being to finance these sometimes astronomically expensive transformations. And in certain aspects, it must be admitted that this passion for redecoration and reconstruction recalls the enthusiasm of the twelfth- and thirteenth-century cathedral crusade.

Disregarding these examples of destruction brought about in the name of taste, the real question is whether or not contemporary society, speaking of "good" and "bad" taste with the same haughty assurance that the eighteenth century spoke of *grand goût* and *petit goût,* is committing similar monumental mistakes. It is not at all unlikely that a twentieth-century art lover, suddenly finding himself in the twelfth century before the façade of Saint-Denis, where all the sculpture was painted with strong – even violent – colors, would exclaim with horror, "What miserable taste!" To avoid this, twentieth-century restorers have decided to leave the stone bare, and in so doing have violated without the slightest misgiving the thought of Cluny, Suger, and the cathedral builders.

THE CREATIVE OUTBURST

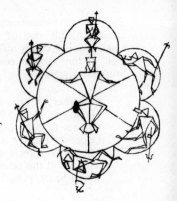

There is no need to emphasize that the true point of departure of the cathedral crusade is to be found in the religious faith of the Middle Ages. Circumstances were particularly favorable to the flowering of such architectural manifestations of piety. It goes without saying that if the Middle Ages had not been pre-eminently a pious age, the builders' genius and the merchants' money would have been used in other ways, and there would be no Chartres, no Amiens, no Strasbourg. . . . Thus, when one insists on Suger's pride of authorship and the vanity of the bourgeois spirit – psychological factors as important in their own way as the technical and economic events to be discussed – one must not lose sight of the spiritual background against which these characteristics were traced.

Space limitations permit only the most cursory mention of this background. Many works from the beginning of the romantic period to the present have given richly detailed pictures of it. Certainly, a much more precise picture could be painted even with certain important retouchings, but only in a more extensive work than this, to include a study of theology, philosophy, and various traditional hermetic sciences, alchemy, astrology, etc. The only specific spiritual point to be taken up here is the increasing force of devotion to the Virgin Mary in the Middle Ages, since this devotion had a powerful

37

effect on the construction of cathedrals. St. Bernard, unquestionably one of the pivotal figures of medieval Christianity, lent his influence to the development of the Cult of the Virgin,[3] celebrated at the time in beautiful liturgical hymns:

O salutary Virgin, Star of the Sea,
Having as a child the sun of Equity,
Creator of light, O ever Virgin, accept our praise.
Queen of Heaven, through whom the sick are cured,
The devoted receive Grace, the afflicted Joy, and
The world the celestral light and hope of salvation;
Royal heart, pure Virgin, grant us thy care and thy
[protection,
Receive our wishes and by thy prayers relieve all
[pain. *

The Virgin was nowhere more honored and venerated than at Notre-Dame de Chartres. A tradition claims that on the site of the cathedral was a grotto where a child-bearing virgin was secretly worshiped a century before the birth of Christ. Some of the Virgin's more remarkable relics were piously preserved at Chartres, among them the garment she wore the night Christ was born. In the fire of 1194 this precious relic was miraculously saved, as was her blue window – of a blue unequalled in the thirteenth century. This masterpiece, now called *Notre-Dame de la Belle Verrière* (Our Lady of the Beautiful Glass), was installed in the choir in the thirteenth century.

At Notre-Dame de Senlis, the story of the Virgin occupies the central portal. At Notre-Dame de Paris, two portals are reserved for representations of her. At Reims, her statue is on the trumeau of the central portal. The Cistercians put their churches under the Virgin's special protection, and during the twelfth century most of the great churches were dedicated to Our Lady – Laon, Paris, Amiens. [4]

The enthusiasm for cathedral building began during the second thirty years of the twelfth century: at Sens about 1130, Noyon in 1151, in Laon in 1160, in Paris

---

* English translation from Coulton, *op. cit.*

38

in 1163. It reached its maximum intensity in the last three decades of the century and the first three of the thirteenth: Chartres in 1194, Bourges by 1195, Rouen in 1200, Mans in 1217, Reims in 1211, Amiens in 1221, and Beauvais in 1247. This enthusiasm sustained itself for one generation, long enough for the work on these buildings to get well under way; then, little by little, the passionate interest in construction fell off and, although work continued, it was less active in the last third of the thirteenth century and the first decades of the fourteenth. For all practical purposes, the Hundred Years' War, beginning in 1337, closed the workshops, and despite renewed efforts at the end of the war, in 1453, no French cathedral was ever completely finished.

These great cathedrals form a crown around Notre-Dame de Paris, running from Reims in the east to Mans in the west, and from Laon and Amiens in the north to Bourges in the south. [5] These cities in which cathedrals were built were episcopal sees. Toward the end of the fifth century the Church decided which Gallo-Roman cities would become episcopal sees. Most of them were located south of the Massif Central, in those parts of Gaul which were then more highly developed economically and more heavily populated than the rest of the country. Grasse, Vence, and Antibes at that time were bishoprics, as were such cities as Riez and Senez, now forgotten towns located in the Basse-Alpes, one of the most disinherited and sparsely populated departments in France.

As the Middle Ages gained impetus, other regions of ancient Gaul, in general, developed with the greatest spiritual and economic vigor. During this phase of the growth of Christianity the cities cited above were episcopal cities without the financial means to build large cathedrals. The word "cathedral" usually evokes the image of a great church building, while in fact many cathedrals were very modest undertakings. Conversely, many parish churches in prosperous regions were ambitiously conceived and much larger than numerous cathedrals. Here "cathedral" [6] is used – in contradistinction to "monastic church" – to indicate parish churches as well as cathedral churches per se.

The history of cathedral construction and the builders

is directly related to the revival of free cities and commerce, to the birth of a middle class and the first urban freedoms. In the early Middle Ages, urban life diminished, little by little, merchants disappeared, municipal organization died. Technical knowledge that had survived from antiquity fell into disuse; if only a few men had carefully preserved the secret of stonecutting, it would not have taken several centuries of groping to discover a satisfactory new system.

Strictly speaking, there were no cities left, only fortified castles. Europe became an agricultural continent in

which all wealth lay in the land. Western economy bogged down and national income reached its lowest ebb. Then, beginning in the tenth century, a relative peace was established: profit-seeking vagabonds and displaced adventurers began transporting goods from one corner of Europe to the other, thus re-establishing commerce. These men installed themselves at the confluences of rivers or at important crossroads, and their activity helped cities to revive. Farsighted landowners contacted these energetic groups and encouraged them to establish towns.

The great Belgian medievalist Henri Pirenne has been struck by the parallel between events of the eleventh and twelfth centuries in Europe and those of the American Far West in the nineteenth century. Similarities between new towns of the eleventh and twelfth centuries and pre-planned towns designed by nineteenth-century American businessmen to follow the development of the railroad are striking. Both hoped to attract settlers by the most favorable material and personal conditions. Publicity was used to lure settlers. The charter of a newly founded city was circulated throughout the countryside, and, just as today, the press published the most attractive prospectus on the resources, charm, and possibilities of the "town" being formed.

There is yet another parallel to be drawn between Europe – especially eleventh- and twelfth-century France – and nineteenth- and twentieth-century America. It is extremely interesting to study the curve of American economics and psychology because it follows a development similar to that of medieval Europe. It is both reassuring and terrifying to see history repeating itself so closely. Medieval economy bloomed with this freedom of work and free competition. There was an important increase in personal property values: joint stock companies and corporate societies were established. Commercial growth gave birth to money changers, bankers, and industrialists. But the Church, opposed to the idea of profit, was able to make these profiteers feel guilty and obtain pardon by donating or bequeathing some of their wealth to such pious works as church construction. Thus a powerful means of financing cathedrals was established: a man gives much more willingly when he has amassed a large fortune.

From the first, the mode of life in these urban groups contrasted with that of a society living solely from the land. Laws that regulated an agarian society were unsatisfactory controls over these commercial newcomers, who frequently rioted with arms to set up a municipal organization and win legal and administrative automony. Out of these riots came the first communes – legal associations sanctioned by royal charters. The oldest commune north

Chartres, window: the money-changers

of the Alps is Cambrai, dating from 1077, and the communal movement extended to other cities such as Sens, Noyon, Laon, Rouen, Reims, Amiens, and Beauvais. Other cities (Paris, for example) were not subject to taxation. And all these cities built great cathedrals.

As noted above, there was a close relationship between the commercial strength of the cities, their independence, and ecclesiastical construction. Nearly all the cities that gained urban independence were located on important overland or river trade routes. In the Massif Central, a region relatively difficult to cross, there were few communes or large cathedrals. The situation was similar in Brittany, which lay outside the important trade routes and in which no communes or cathedrals were found in the twelfth and thirteenth centuries.

The spirit of the medieval bourgeois played a decisive role in the cathedral crusade because it was inspired by a deep local patriotism. Proud of having wrested his freedom from the feudal lord, he wanted the Church and city to know his joy – nothing was so marvelous or so important! The city was his, and he wanted to impress strangers with the magnificence of his churches. A young nation's enthusiasm is often expressed in colossal and immeasurable ways. It was young Egypt that built the pyramids, works of the first dynasties. The United States has surpassed all previous records [for tall buildings] by building skyscrapers higher and higher. The Empire State Building culminated this drive for height with its 102 floors, a total height of 1472 feet.

This young medieval society was symbolized by its bourgeois. His enthusiasm permeated by a desire to break records, he constantly raised his cathedral naves higher and higher. In 1163, Notre-Dame de Paris began its record construction to result in a vault 114 feet 8 inches from the floor. Chartres surpassed Paris in 1194, eventually reaching 119 feet 9 inches. In 1212 Reims started to rise to 124 feet 3 inches, and in 1221 Amiens reached 138 feet 9 inches. This drive to break records reached its climax in 1247 with the project to vault the choir of Beauvais 157 feet 3 inches above the floor – only to have the vaults collapse in 1284.

By this time the Middle Ages was reaching maturity.

The middle class was becoming less dynamic, the desire to break records burned out. When Saint-Urban de Troyes – a glass building – was built, it was conceived in a new spirit. Today the United States is in the same situation. The industrial middle class, although unwilling to admit it, is lethargic. A new nation's desire to set records no longer interests it. The celebrated Lever Building, constructed on New York's Park Avenue in 1953, is a glass structure, but only thirty stories high. It symbolizes a turning point in the American psychology.

Bourgeois civic pride, the desire to conquer new worlds, and merchants' vexed souls all contributed to the success of the cathedral crusade. But there were other factors that contributed to the financing of these edifices. From the middle of the twelfth century, the idea of going to the Holy Land was no longer as popular as it has been earlier. Why? Because Jerusalem had been in Christian hands since 1099? Because no one realized the constant menace the Moslems presented to France? Because everyone remembered the difficulties of the First Crusade? Because the taste for luxury and riches began to spread? The Church always authorized those in charge of the fabric to grant indulgences to anyone helping to build God's House. It was no longer necessary to go on a crusade to atone for sins. The cathedral crusade took form, and the entire ecclesiastical hierarchy from Pope to simple parish priest contributed to it spiritually and financially.

Following the disasters of the poorly organized expeditions of 1147, 1187, and 1204, crusades to defend or recapture Christ's Tomb became an idea of the past. The difficulties that confronted St. Louis when he tried to organize his army in the mid-thirteenth century are characteristic of the spiritual state of the time. In might be said that the cathedral crusade contributed to the weakening of the French kingdom.

Contrary to what is generally believed, the cathedral crusade met resistance of its own. Pious, influential men were scandalized by such extensive undertakings. Petrus Cantor, one of the high dignitaries of Notre-Dame de Paris, wrote vehemently in 1180: "... This lust for building is testified to by the palaces of princes, erected

from the tears and the money wrung from the poor."
He compared it to a disease, a raging epidemic: "But
monastic or ecclesiastical edifices are raised from the
usury and breed of barren metal among covetous men,
from the lying deceits and deceitful lies of hireling
preachers." * Petrus had little of the effect on cathedral
construction that St. Bernard had on the luxury of Cluny
and Saint-Denis, and although his denouncement may
have been prompted by wisdom, it had little effect on the
ardor and emotion that activated the workshops.

God's House was the earthly image of the Heavenly
Jerusalem, and it was a beautiful thing: it was the house
of adoration, the house of the people. In most ancient
religions, the people did not have access to the sanctuary.
But the Christian church, by contrast, demanded that her
faithful contribute to the construction of churches large
enough for the populace to have access. Ecclesiastical
law emphasized the difference between the sanctuary and
the remaining area of the cathedral. During the Middle
Ages, Notre-Dame de Paris belonged not to the bishop,
but to the chapter whose jurisdiction ended at the sanctuary, which was reserved for the bishop, as was true for
all cathedral sanctuaries. Naves and side aisles were
reserved especially for worshipers, that is, for the people. [7]
This distinction is important because, otherwise, the
twentieth-century spirit is likely to be offended by the
worldly activities that went on inside these medieval
churches. People slept, ate, talked openly, and brought
animals – dogs and falcons – inside. Circulation was
much freer than now because there were no chairs. Often
the most secular matters were discussed inside the
churches. Communal representatives met in the cathedral
to discuss city business, and it has been noted that in some
of the communes with large cathedrals the burghers did
not even build a city hall. There is at least one text
forbidding a commune to use the cathedral as a meeting
hall, proof enough that it was a common occurrence. It
was evidently not a right in itself, but simply tolerated
by the Church. At Marseille, meetings of the guild
masters, councils, and business leaders were regularly
held in the Church of the Major. Presumably, communal

* English translation from Coulton, *op. cit.*

representatives helped finance the city cathedral with the idea of holding their meetings there. If this supposition is disturbing it must be remembered that these men lived in daily contact with the divinity. They were probably much less intimidated by the Lord than the modern Christian who encounters God at best every Sunday morning in his parish church.

Following this line of thought, account must be taken of professional organizations who did not consider it disrespectful to make announcements in the Cathedral of Chartres. Examining the church closely, it becomes evident that the guilds obtained the best possible placement for their windows. They are installed along the side aisles or in the ambulatory nearest the public, while glass donated by bishops and lords was relegated to the clerestory windows of the nave and choir. The cloth merchant, the stonecutter, the wheelwright, and the carpenter each had himself depicted in a medallion in the lower part of the window donated by his guild, as close as possible, as it were, to future clients.

Numerous feasts increased the contact between God and medieval man, explaining in part the latter's passion for enlarging and beautifying his church. Never has a civilization offered so many holidays to its peasants and workers. In February, 1956, France voted three weeks of annual vacation plus ten legal feast days for every citizen, and in so doing became the world's first country to give its citizens anything approximating that granted by the Church in the Middle Ages. It should be remembered that in former times the working day was much longer than today. Frequently it began at dawn and ended at sundown. The number of annual feasts varied according to the year and town in question. In fifty-two weeks, there was an average of thirty feast days, noted in workshop accounts. In the accounts of the Cistercian abbey at Vale Royal, England, in 1280, twenty-nine feast days are specified. Idle days brought no pay in the Middle Ages, although today employers are legally bound to give pay on some feast days.

The working population quit work at noon on Saturdays and all feast days. Adding all these half-days to feast days, it would seem that the medieval laborer

Chartres, window: stonecutters

averaged only a five-day week. This is proved by the detailed account of the workshop at the Augustinian convent in Paris in 1299. Workers, hired by the day, were generally paid for five days per week, never more and occasionally less:

Expenditures for the second week of August:

    To Master Robert for 5 days . . . 10 s.

    To 3 masons, each for 5 days . . . 29 s. 2 d.

    To 5 assistants, each for 5 days . . . 24 s. 7 d.

Expenditures for the third week of August:

    To Master Robert for 5 days . . . 10 s.

Expenditures for the fourth week of August:

    To Master Robert for 4 days . . . 8 s.

    To Jean de Saint-Quentin, to Girart de
Van..., to Guillaume, stonecutters,
each for 4 days at 2 sous per day . . 24 s.

Expenditures for the second week of September:

    To Master Robert for 5 days . . . 10 s.

    To 2 assistants and a scaffolder, each
for 5 days . . . . 15 s. 10 d.

This account eloquently proves that the medieval working population was not overburdened with work. Indeed, it ought to be envied rather than pitied, for its leisure was magnificently organized by the authorities and absolutely free. It is not unlikely that the medieval laborer's leisure had a considerable influence on the cathedral crusade and the work of enlarging the churches.

The Church masterfully organized ceremonies and processions. One can only try to imagine the splendor of medieval religious feasts. Probably only the services in St. Peter's in Rome adequately recall those of the past. On important feast days, ecclesiastical authorities concentrated their efforts on ceremonies in the cathedral, to the detriment of those taking place in parish churches. The congregations from various parishes usually wanted to attend the services in the cathedral. This is analogous to the situation today when it is announced that an international soccer match is to be played in a city's largest stadium. On the big day, the population rushes to the game *en masse*, abandoning local stadiums in which matches of only sectional importance are being played. Thus those stadiums scheduling international matches must be as large as possible. For comparable reasons – *mutatis mutandis* – the medieval cathedral had to be sufficiently large to accommodate crowds coming from every part of the city. Faced with an influx of the faithful, authorities were constantly pressed to enlarge their cathedrals. The area of some was increased to handle a larger number of worshipers than the total inhabitants of the city, space being opened for peasants from neighboring parish churches.

When the bourgeois and his wife left their small house – their windows and doors locked – and set out slowly through the narrow, tortuous streets to the feast, the cathedral towers and spires seen over the city roofs seemed to him much taller and attenuated than to us today. The area of the city was limited by surrounding fortifications, and the land inside the boundary in great demand and expensive. For this reason houses were built right up to the cathedral walls. There was hardly any open area, and in the Middle Ages a cathedral could never be admired from a distance as it can be today. The frame constituted by old houses has most often been destroyed. Notre-Dame de Paris has the most disproportionate square of all. Napoleon III, fearing that in the event of a future revolution rioters could easily barricade themselves in the narrow Cité streets, had that part of the island razed. The loss of this old topography is regrettable, but it is fortunate that we can now examine the cathedral without having to contend with the noise and disorder of the immense workshop. Much to his sorrow, the medieval bourgeois never saw his cathedral completed. He could only hope that some day his son would see the end of that eternal chaos in the workshop. All the guilds worked in an area surrounded by carts carrying construction materials; there were sculptors, stonecutters, masons, plasterers, roofers, scaffolders, smiths, overseers, plumbers, painters, and artisans of many other crafts. The scaffolding attached to the wall always hid a part of the building.

The bourgeois, watching this spectacular activity, had the satisfaction of judiciously controlling the funds he had provided. He was doubtless thus encouraged to be even more generous when extra funds were needed. What seventeenth-century bourgeois would have given a part of his wealth to an absolute monarch?

The curious or devout passer-by, approaching the portal, enjoyed recognizing sculptured figures of Old and

New Testament characters close to his heart and soul. The thing that made the Middle Ages moving and amicable was this: the lettered and the ignorant had the same book of images, and they received the same education, the only difference being one of degree. Several centuries later it was different. The educated man of the Renaissance, in cultivating antiquity to excess, had mythological scenes painted and sculpted that were simply incomprehensible to the general public. The introduction of the humanities abruptly separated the masses from men of learning – a situation that to this day has not been completely rectified in western Europe.

Advancing into the church, the bourgeois found other familiar scenes. Until about the middle of the twelfth century, the book of images opened itself on frescoed walls and vaults, as in Saint-Savin, for example. Then, little by little, windows became larger as wall space contracted, providing light but limiting the opportunity to paint large frescoes. After that time, the book of images was inscribed in the beautiful stained glass windows.

Under the cathedral vaults – another aspect of medieval harmony – men of all social conditions met side by side. The bourgeois found the peasant as well as the

Saint-Savin, fresco: construction of the Tower of Babel

bishop, the nobleman, and even the king. The great men of the realm came to pray in the cathedral and gave generously for its munificence. The era was yet to come when the wealthy faithful would consecrate their money to the construction of luxurious private chapels, even though a number existed in the thirteenth century and the tradition of private chapels can be traced to the late eighth century.

This union of both religious and secular classes under the aegis of the Church could be found solemnly expressed in plain sight, engraved in a circular plaque imbedded in the labyrinth of the nave. On this were

Chartres: the labyrinth

found the names and portraits of those responsible for building the church.

Beside the portrait of the bishop those of the architects were incised. These labyrinths were thought to represent the pilgrimage route in the Holy Land, and this symbolic relationship was so strong in the belief of the time that a trip over the maze carried with it the same grace and indulgences as a pilgrimage itself. This seems curious perhaps, and gives an unexpected importance to the builders, but it must not be forgotten that ideas borrowed from the vocabulary of architecture have always held a high place in Christian symbolism – for example, the evangelical term "cornerstone" and the title, *Pontifix Maximus,* taken from the Romans (*pontifix* being a bridge builder).

Only one of these labyrinths is extant today, that at Chartres (59 feet in diameter). The origin of this type of design must perhaps be sought in Cretan civilization, or, possibly, it was introduced into western Europe by megalithic society, for there is in the entrance to the Dublin Museum a magnificent megalithic labyrinth incised in stone. Piously, on their knees, the faithful followed the maze to reach the center of the labyrinth where the symbolic plaque was located. None of these plaques remain today, but the inscriptions on two of them are known – those of Amiens and Reims. The former reads:

In the year of Grace 1220, the work on this church was begun. The bishop of this diocese was at that time Evrard; the king of France, Louis [VIII], son of Philip Augustus. The master of works was named Master Robert de Luzarches, after him came Thomas de Cormont, and, after the latter, his son Renaud who had this inscription made in the year of the Incarnation 1288.

The portraits of the bishop and the three architects were incised in white marble. The highest dignitaries of the Church and great feudal lords, as well as the peasant and bourgeois, having covered the maze on their knees, saw the names and faces of these men of genius, and often of humble origin, who had dared conceive this

53

extraordinary architecture. What higher honor could have been paid the cathedral builders? Today's architects and planners are far from having such glory. These plaques constitute a weighty argument against the thesis

of the anonymity of the medieval architect. The honor
of having his name inscribed in God's House inspired
him to do great things, demonstrating the wisdom of the
Church in authorizing these inscriptions.

THE CANON-BUILDERS

Cathedral construction cannot be understood without knowledge of the singularly important role of the cathedral chapters. Stories have come down about the deeds of various bishops in elaborating the plans and financing of the great enterprise, undertakings that are unquestionably true. Indeed, many cathedrals owe much recognition to their bishops: Notre-Dame de Paris must be associated with Maurice de Sully and his efforts on its behalf, Senlis owes much to Thibaut, and Amiens much to Evrard. It is only a legend that bishops did *not* play an essential role in the development of their cathedrals. But the bishop was only a star who burned brightly and then disappeared from the scene, while cathedral construction programs continued from one generation to another. Under whose care? Who maintained a cathedral? It was the chapter. Moreover, medieval cathedrals belonged more often to the chapters than to the bishops. Hugues de Bourgogne donated land on which to build the cathedral at Autun not to the bishop but to the chapter.

The meaning of this word "chapter" must be clarified first, because it no longer has the meaning it did in the Middle Ages. Since the French Revolution, the role of the chapter has been much more honorary than active, but in medieval times the chapter was an assembly of canons who enjoyed great privileges and who were frequently outside episcopal jurisdiction. Only at the Council of Trent in the sixteenth century was its relationship to the bishop defined. Canons were the true ca-

57

thedral builders, and they must be brought out of obscurity and given their due honor, for it was they who directed the cathedral crusade and who sustained work through the centuries, often from their own revenue when public enthusiasm had long been dead.

What was the historical origin of the chapter? And how was this assembly able to take such a place in the temporal direction of the Church? In the early Middle Ages each bishop had under him a body of priests who assisted him in administrating his diocese and saying Mass in its parishes. It was in regulating his priests' lives that Bishop Chrodegang of Metz (742-766) instituted canonical law. His canons – in a certain sense his privy council – were forced into a communal life, to live under his canonical rules. Henceforth they slept in dormitories, had a common refectory, and celebrated their offices as a community.

At Aix-la-Chapelle in 817, Louis the Pious, having made certain that the canons would take vows of obedience and chastity, practically annulled the vow of poverty. This was to have important consequences. Canons legally had life tenure on their lodgings and could dispose of their movable property by bequest. This decision gradually led canons to break with their communal existence and return to a more secular and individualistic life.

Beginning in the first half of the tenth century, several cathedral chapters had their revenues separated from those of the bishops. From then on, chapter independence grew. Chapters now dispensed with a common treasury and each canon was given a prebend, that is, a more or less important ecclesiastical revenue. Prebends did not oblige the canons to live in the cathedral city, and some were even able to control several prebends located in other dioceses. In short, there were resident and nonresident canons. The establishment of a dean at the head of the chapter resulted in further freedom from episcopal control. The chapter included a certain number of officers: a chancellor who acted as secretary and who was responsible for the seals, a treasurer in charge of the treasury and relics, and a cantor who was the choirmaster and who directed the chant and organized the religious services. Following the *ceremoniale episcoporum,* canons took precedent over mitered priests.

As cities grew and the population increased, more canons were appointed. Commercial developments and improved agricultural methods increased prebend values which in turn increased the power of the chapters. Canons gradually increased their rights and privileges, becoming jealous of their authority and even anxious to limit the bishop's power. Legal disputes became increasingly frequent and were generally settled in favor of these powerful assemblies, as for example at Notre-Dame de Paris in 1335. The bishop himself was forced to concede in an act of November 5, that the dean, the chapter, and each of the individual canons, "members of the choir of Notre-Dame and all their domestics" were exempt from his jurisdiction and should denounce his lawyers or counselors if they said otherwise.

In all cathedrals the chapter controlled the fabric. In the Middle Ages, "fabric" was understood to mean everything pertaining to the construction or maintenance of the cathedral, both in its physical execution and in the acquisition and administration of the funds affected by it. The bishop seems rarely to have been consulted or to have taken any responsibility in the fabric. When he did, it was with full willingness and an exceptional honor.

In developing plans and seeing to their execution, the chapter played a part comparable to that of the modern city planning commission. The same order of problems had to be solved: expropriation, financing, contracts, all of which presented difficulties similar to those involved

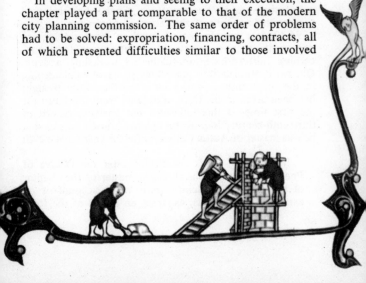

in any large project today. Then as now, individual interests opposed general goals and complicated the job from the outset. Expropriation always occasioned bitter fights. The builders of Amiens Cathedral in the thirteenth century were prevented from working by the obstinacy of a religious community. Between 1230 and 1240 brothers of the hospital at Amiens simply could not (or were unwilling to) understand that the city wanted to enlarge its cathedral at the expense of the neighboring hospital. Their ill will made it necessary, in order to obtain their permission, to pay large indemnities over and above rebuilding their hospital near a large waterway at the chapter's expense. They were paid one hundred livres a year for five years and an impartial four-man commission was set up to determine the cost of dismantling the hospital. Measures also had to be taken to prevent strong arguments between those brothers who were willing to move and those determined to stay. The latter were continually begged to concede to the wishes of the city's clergy and people. Today's expropriated villagers are not unlike these thirteenth-century ecclesiastics.

Canons were to meet at the beginning of each year to select a master, a person whose task was to keep the fabric accounts and to oversee the workshop. The master might be a canon or a priest or, very rarely, a lay agent responsible to the chapter, chosen for his knowledge of architecture and his business sense. Chance has preserved the detailed account of the fabric at Autun for the year 1294-1295, a simple record worth a thousand literary documents because it reveals an infinity of facts concerning thirteenth-century cathedral workshop activity. Quicherat studied this marvelous piece of bookkeeping in the nineteenth century, but since then little thought has been given to it. Here, translated from the Latin for the first time, is this unknown but amazing record of thirteenth-century life. Robert Clavel himself tells us that he was master of Autun Cathedral for the year 1294-1295:

In the year 1295, the Friday after the Octave of Pentecost, Robert Clavel, clerk, master of the chapter of the Church of Saint-Lazare, made account of all expenses and receipts, expenses on behalf of the fore-

named chapter since the Monday after the Octave of Pentecost of the year 1294, to Sunday in the Octave of Pentecost in this said year 1295, deduction of 12 livres 11 deniers being made as payment. Without forgetting to deduct the advance received in view of these expenses, it remains that the chapter of Autun owes this said Robert 53 Vienne livres 6 sous 3 deniers, the sum that this said Robert owed to the chapter of Autun according to the count made this Monday.

Quicherat analyzed these Clavel accounts and determined that they fall into seven catagories: (1) assessments on the chapter at Autun; (2) revenues from vacant benefices in the city and diocese that by papal permission could be devoted to the cathedral fabric; (3) receipts of indulgences granted to benefactors of the fabric; (4) receipts of the quest by the confraternity of Saint-Lazare during Pentecost; (5) receipts of surplus revenues: the chapter took in benefices not devoted to the fabric, which amounted to 34 livres 19 sous 5 deniers. There were several bequests by individuals from other places, among them a lady from Cluny, but donors generally belonged to the diocese of Autun and were peasants save one, Master Humbertus de Virgultis, whose name indicates that he was a clerk. The curates of Buxy and Saffres brought in 5 sous 9 deniers and 14 sous from renting plows in their parishes, and the village of Marcheseul, which belonged to the chapter, furnished 12 sous 2 deniers; (6) receipts from alms-boxes set up especially to benefit the fabric – one at the home of Isabelle Raclete, at the curate's of Autun, at Martinet the draper, at Grimoard's, at Robin the goldsmith and boxmaker, at Gilles Gododin's in Saint-Pancrace of Autun, at Saint-Jean de la Crotte, and in the church at Bligny – in all, 10 livres 17 sous 2 deniers; (7) the chapter deduction totaling 42 livres 13 sous 3 deniers which had been subtracted from the donations to the Autun Cathedral from Pentecost 1294 to Pentecost 1295. The total of the stated accounts received before the last article came to 400 livres 9 sous 9 deniers.

These were the expenditures:

In the quarries, for extracting stones intended for the upkeep of the Church of Saint-Lazare . . .	8 l.	10 s.	4 d.
To the same [places] for the year's lime	9 l.	8 s.	
For cutting and transporting wood for centering at the Church of Saint-Lazare, and for carpenters and laborers	17 l.	2 s.	7 d.

To the forge at Autun, for the year	42 l.	10 s.	6 d.
To the forge at the quarry, 62 sous, including our iron	3 l.	2 s.	
To laborers for working this said quarry	4 l.	15 s.	4 d.
For study of the quarry site at Marmontain	1 l.	10 s.	
To laborers who put on the roof tiles at the Church of Saint-Lazare	1 l.	9 s.	11 d.
For poles used		5 s.	
For making and reinforcing 12 wagons with iron	1 l.	15 s.	
To carpenters for wood cut in the chapter's forest	8 l.	16 s.	
For repairing the roof of the Church of Saint-Lazare and emplacement of the machines required, for carpenters and laborers . . .	3 l.	15 s.	
To carpenters who sheeted the Church of Saint-Lazare	10 l.	8 s.	
To buy the sheeting		3 s.	6 d.

For the nails and other iron pieces required for the construction of the sanctuary of the Church of Saint-Lazare . . . .   16 s.   8 d.

To Master Pierre de Dijon, tiler .   70 l.

To this said Pierre 12 livres were paid in the preceding account . .
Expenses incurred in transporting the stones known as "gargoyles" .   4 l.   10 s.   9 d.

To Renaud, tavern-keeper, for rent of the house in which this present master [Pierre] lives, for two terms of the present year . . . .   3 l.

For clothing for this said master, the quarter's rent of the Nativity of St. John the Baptist not included .   10 l.

For iron pegs, iron-bound grinding wheels, and iron itself   . . .   18 s.   3 d.

For making the roofers' hammers   1 s.   10 d.

To the harness-maker Benoit for yokes, collars, halters, and other leather articles necessary for the wagon . . . .   2 l.   10 s.

For hay, and for the yoke required for the wagon . . . . .   19 l.   17 s.   4 d.

For oats	25 l.	3 s.	9 d.
For horseshoes	4 l.	6 s.	
For the nails and iron used to strengthen the new wagons and repair the old	6 l.	9 s.	1 d.
To the wheelwright for the year, for the new wagons and repair of the old	2 l.	14 s.	9 d.
For axle grease, oil, vinegar, and 30 pound of candles, for the year .	2 l.	7 s.	
Rent, charges, and expenses of a wagon	18 l.		
For the rent of carriages, stables, and a loft	2 l.		
For rope			13 d.
For care of a horse		5 s.	
To buy a horse for the wagon . .	3 l.	10 s.	

A master like Robert Clavel – in addition to providing the workshop with first-class workers and manufactured products – had to direct the transport of materials, oversee the workers, assure the continuance of all religious services despite the work, and organize the maintenance of completed buildings.

In 1295 Clavel succeeded in balancing his budget, but often workshop expenses exceeded chapter revenues. Incoming funds were insufficient to cover the cost of the materials used and to pay the workers, who would then leave that city to find work in another shop. In such situations canons busied themselves finding new resources to resume work. Their success proved them the equals of modern ministers of finance with their unbalanced national budgets. They addressed themselves to confessors, instructing them to remind their faithful that dishonestly gained goods must be turned over to the fabric. They incited the young religious confraternities established to assist in aiding the fabric – such as that at Saint-Lazare at Autun – to a more energetic effort in organizing their collections. Clerics who arrived later for religious services were fined. From the pulpit orators expounded the spiritual gifts to be accorded benefactors of the cathedral:

> Noble and kind gentlemen [said an orator of Amiens in 1260], you can be twenty-seven days closer to Paradise than you were yesterday if sin, envy, and lust do not cost you this indulgence and, moreover, with it you can draw near again to the souls of your fathers, mothers, and all those whom you love best.

In addition to all this, chapters decided that anyone desiring to be buried within the walls of the church would have to pay for the privilege. Finally, when the need was acute, canons taxed themselves heavily. And, too, bishops often contributed considerable funds to the fabric in difficult times.

One of the most efficient means of collecting funds was the public exhibition of relics. Fortunate indeed were the churches with important and celebrated relics. At Laon, in 1112, three months after a fire had ravaged the cathedral, seven canons and several layman left the

Recovery of a child before coffer containing the relics of Saint Louis (beginning of the fifteenth century)

city with the relics saved from the fire – a piece of the Virgin's veil, a fragment of the Holy Sponge, and a part of the True Cross – to visit Issoudun, Tours, Angers, Le Mans, and Chartres. They returned in the fall with funds they hoped to be sufficient for reconstructing their cathedral; but these funds were quickly drained away, and by the spring of 1113 it was decided to organize a second tour, this time to England. Going through Arras and Saint-Omer, the canons embarked for England at Wissant. Their crossing was by no means easy, for these pious voyagers were robbed by Flemish merchants and attacked by pirates. Yet they arrived safely in Dover and visited Canterbury, Winchester, Salisbury, and Exeter. They returned at the end of September with sufficient funds for their cathedral to be consecrated on August 29, 1114.

But the cult of relics led to abuses. Some relics of very doubtful authenticity were exhibited. In the face of these excesses the Church showed its concern at the Lateran Council in 1215 by forbidding veneration of any object without express permission. After this date the adoration of relics faltered in intensity, and in the Autun accounts, for example, no further mention of funds raised in this manner is made. However, abuses continued: in the *fabliaux* and, later, in Boccaccio, sharp indignation is expressed against certain clerical stratagems which could not always be readily differentiated from pure and simple swindling. This indignation, becoming an open revolt, would one day become one of the causes of the Reformation.

Apocalypse (late thirteenth century)

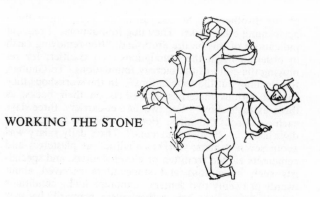

WORKING THE STONE

In the hierarchy of cathedral builders, the laborer was evidently at the bottom of the scale, but every opportunity was open to him to advance himself as long as the ascendant period of the Middle Ages lasted. With hard work and intelligence he could become a specialist. He might save a little money and establish himself as a contractor or, by studying, train himself to take up the duties of an architect. Medieval society allowed the most humble men to reach high positions. The future belonged to the ambitious. The evolution of the medieval working world presents a certain analogy to that in America. All things being equal, the medieval laborer could become a self-made man and assume an estimable position in his city.

These laborers were recruited from the uprooted "class." They were often serfs who had fled from their masters, seeking refuge in cities far from their native regions. If they were not reclaimed by their masters within a year and a day, they became free and citizens of the city. Laborers were also probably recruited from the peasantry, the sons of large families seeking adventure and freedom in the city. They were all able to find jobs immediately in one of the many city workshops. Workers in these workshops were freemen.

Various tasks were demanded of laborers. The Autun accounts show that they assisted carpenters in transporting timber, excavated to open a quarry, and carried slate for the roof of Saint-Lazare. The accounts of the Monastery

71

of the Brothers of St. Augustine in Paris show them performing other tasks. They dug foundations. Frequent indications of this nature are found: "For removing earth in order to begin the foundations. To Gautier, for removing the earth of the sacristy foundations. To Gautier, for cleaning out the foundations." In the workshops they carried various materials in baskets on their backs, as these extracts show: "For two basket-carriers, three days each . . . 3 sous 6 deniers. For seven basket-carriers, five days each . . . 20 sous 5 deniers." Their daily salary was about seven deniers; workers qualified as plasterers and cementers earned from ten or eleven deniers, and specialists such as masons and stonecutters received about twenty or twenty-two deniers. Laborers' living conditions must therefore have been rather severe, primarily because work was irregular and salaries low.

It is difficult to reconcile the presence of these laborers in the workshops with the legend about volunteer labor, an episodic phenomenon which could have held only a negligible place in construction. Free work literally took bread out of the mouths of laborers in search of work. The only work unskilled laborers might perform was to carry materials or dig foundations, and they must have taken a dim view of those who offered to work for nothing. The *chanson de geste* of the four Aymon sons tells the legendary story of a nobleman, Renaud de Montauban, who, to atone for his sins, joined a workshop where he accepted only a pittance. After a week the regular workers became concerned about this man who was causing their wages to be lowered. They decided to do away with him and, attacking him from behind, beat him to death with axes and threw his body in the Rhine. But their crime did not go unpunished. Happily, the fish gathered together and lifted his body which floated with the current, lighted by three candles. This story symbolized the workers' hostility to unremunerated work by the zealous and the faithful.

Specialists and professionals attached to themselves a number of laborers to assist them in their tasks, the latter being called variously aides, servants, companions, or valets. The Autun accounts studied in the preceding chapter provide information about this:

72

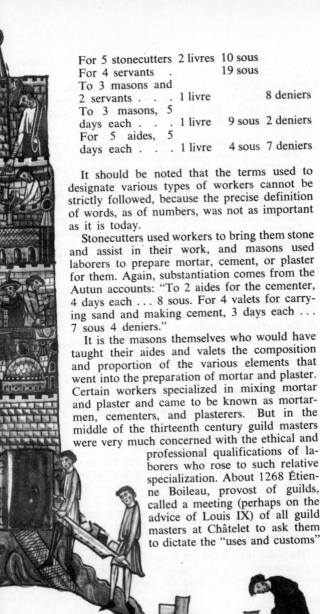

For 5 stonecutters	2 livres	10 sous	
For 4 servants .		19 sous	
To 3 masons and 2 servants . . .	1 livre		8 deniers
To 3 masons, 5 days each . . .	1 livre	9 sous	2 deniers
For 5 aides, 5 days each . . .	1 livre	4 sous	7 deniers

It should be noted that the terms used to designate various types of workers cannot be strictly followed, because the precise definition of words, as of numbers, was not as important as it is today.

Stonecutters used workers to bring them stone and assist in their work, and masons used laborers to prepare mortar, cement, or plaster for them. Again, substantiation comes from the Autun accounts: "To 2 aides for the cementer, 4 days each . . . 8 sous. For 4 valets for carrying sand and making cement, 3 days each . . . 7 sous 4 deniers."

It is the masons themselves who would have taught their aides and valets the composition and proportion of the various elements that went into the preparation of mortar and plaster. Certain workers specialized in mixing mortar and plaster and came to be known as mortarmen, cementers, and plasterers. But in the middle of the thirteenth century guild masters were very much concerned with the ethical and professional qualifications of laborers who rose to such relative specialization. About 1268 Étienne Boileau, provost of guilds, called a meeting (perhaps on the advice of Louis IX) of all guild masters at Châtelet to ask them to dictate the "uses and customs"

of their trades. Boileau listed 101 professions. The forty-eighth statute, which is of interest here, was that of "masons, stonecutters, plasterers, and cementers," and was dictated by Guillaume de Saint-Patu, the king's master mason. The king gave his favorite architect mastership over the guild:

The king orders, as God has given him good life, that the master Guillaume de Saint-Patu is given mastership over the masons as it pleases him. The said master Guillaume will stay in Paris in the palace lodge and he will protect the above-mentioned trade faithfully and loyally as best he can, for the poor as for the rich and for the weak as for the strong, so long as it pleases the king for him to watch over the above-said trade. And then that master Guillaume took the foresaid oath before the provost of Paris at Châtelet.

The guild master took advantage of this occasion to insure his own rights: "The master who protects the guild for the king is absolved from night-watch because of the service he renders in protecting the guild."

In the sixth paragraph we read that the guild master alone had the right to have two apprentices rather than one. This statute, like the others in the *Book of the Guilds,* opposed fraud and sought to guarantee a high quality in construction:

If the plasterers send plaster to begin the work of any man, the mason who works for the latter to whom the plaster is sent must swear by his oath that the quality of the plaster is good and true and if he has any suspicions or doubts about the measure, he must weigh the plaster or have it weighed before him and if he finds that the measure is not true, the plasterer must pay 5 sous in amends. To wit, 2 sous to the Chapel of Saint-Blaise, 2 sous to the master who protects the guild, and 1 sou to him who will have weighed the plaster.

The guild master did not forget himself. In the following paragraph it is clear that the plasterer alone had to pay for his admission into the guild in Paris:

No one may be a plasterer in Paris unless he pays 5 Parisian sous to the master who protects the profession for the king. When he has paid the five sous he must swear by the saints that he will put nothing in the plaster save lime and that he will give a good and true measure.

Paragraph fourteen forewarns the plasterer that on the second offense an appeal will be made to the provost who will act accordingly:

If the plasterer puts anything else in his plaster than what he should, he must pay 5 sous in amends, he must pay the master for each time that this is done. If the plasterer habitually does this and is unwilling to amend his ways, the master can forbid him use of the guild and if the plasterer does not wish to leave the guild, the master must make it known to the provost of Paris and the provost must make that plasterer foreswear the aforesaid guild.

The use of force and police intervention is taken up in paragraph twenty: "... the master will make it known to the provost of Paris and the provost of Paris will combat it with force."

The cathedral builders paid taxes, and interesting information concerning them may be drawn from the thirteenth-century Paris municipal tax registers. For the year 1292 there are the names and the sums paid by 15,200 contributors subject to the *taille*, parish by parish and street by street. The *taille* was an imposition levied on persons who were neither nobles nor ecclesiastics, or those who did not enjoy some special exemption. The largest entry that year was that from Gandoufle le Lombard for 114 livres 10 sous, and the smallest was that from the "little people," the lowest economic class, for 12 deniers. The roll is strewn with errors in addition that a ten-year-old child would not make today. And yet no one can be accused of fraud since the errors are sometimes for too much and sometimes for too little. This lack of precision, which seems to characterize medieval man and which showed up in his construction, seems offensive to our modern devotion to minutiae, graphs, and statistics. But this lack of accuracy was greatly compensated for by the spirit of synthesis which animated the epoch. Modern man analyzes and specializes – and the consequences of using this mode of thinking exclusively are beginning to be felt.

Again the document as proof:

> The "little people" outside the Porte Saint-Honoré and the parish of Saint-Germain each paid 1 sou.

Guillaume de Laingny, potter	1 sou
Auberi, carpenter	1 sou
Guillaume, shoemaker	1 sou
Jehan Pasquier, mason	1 sou
Robert, thatcher	1 sou
Symon, glassblower	1 sou
Raoul, tapestry-maker	1 sou
etc.	

To find the total taxes paid by these "little people," one had only to count the number of individuals taxed. Yet the result given in the manuscript shows a mistake in addition of 1 livre 19 sous. The manuscript total is 14 livres 4 sous, but Géraud, who studied the document in the nineteenth century, could find only 12 livres 5 sous.

In the register 192 persons connected with the work of stonecutting are listed, divided into the following categories: 104 masons, 12 stonecutters, 36 plasterers, 8 mortarmen, 2 dressers, 18 quarrymen, 7 assistant masons, 3 overseers, 2 roadmakers.

The assignment of taxes paid by plasterers was great, ranging from 12 deniers to 4 livres 12 sous.

Raoul paid	1 sou
Symon paid	2 sous
Ysabel, plasterer	3 sous
Roger paid	4 sous
Houdée, plasterer	5 sous
Colin paid	6 sous
Jehan paid	8 sous
Henri paid	10 sous
Jehan paid	12 sous
Mestre Yves, plasterer	16 sous

Le Roman de la Rose *(fourteenth century)*

Raoul paid	3 livres	10 sous
Dame Mary, plasterer and two children	4 livres	12 sous

Raoul and Dame Mary quite probably owned quarries of gypsum (mineral from which plaster is made), of which there were important deposits in the region about Paris, particularly on the hillsides of Montmartre. Plaster of Paris was in great demand and exported as far as England and, of course, is famous even today.

The names of several women plasterers, cementers and even, very rarely, masons are found in this text, for these were the guilds which, all things considered, were not too physically demanding. Conversely, there is no evidence of women stonecutters or quarry workers. However, Dame Mary, the plasterer who paid 4 livres 12 sous for herself and her two children, was not a worker. She must have inherited the business from her husband. The thirteenth-century woman had more legal rights than the French woman today, restricted as she is by laws adopted from the Roman juridical system. Even married women paid taxes on their own income and in their own name, for example: "Roger the stonecutter . . . 16 sous; his wife . . . 5 sous." A woman was named in contracts signed by her husband and, at his death, she could transact his real estate business directly with the Church. Raingarde, widow of Master Arnoul, stonecutter at Reims, in 1225 sold a house to the Church of Saint-Symphorien and one to Clarambard, a canon at Reims. At the same time she busied herself having this sale ratified by her son Raoulet, at that time a minor, until he reached legal age, for which she gave as guarantee another house located in the Rue Saint-Etienne. The preachers and moralists of the Middle Ages, in slandering women, have masked the active and constructive role they played in that society. The part women played in the success of the cathedral crusade was decisive and should be recognized.

We find among the mortarmen as among the plasterers a great number of taxes:

Marguerite, mortarman	1 sou
Richard, mortarman	2 sous
Robert, mortarman	3 sous
Vincent, mortarman	5 sous
Guerin, mortarman	1 livre
Pierre, mortarman	2 livres

But it must be noted here that the term "mortarman" probably covered two trades. There was in Paris, near the Seine, a street of mortarmaking where the mortarmen's products were found. They worked with lias stone, a hard stone found in the neighborhood of Paris which was without any faults and capable of being highly polished. Theirs was a delicate profession requiring a long apprenticeship. It was to these mortarmakers that statute sixteen of Étienne Bouleau's work was probably addressed: "Mortarmen cannot take an apprentice for less than 6 years' service."

Paragraph twenty-one refers especially to mortarmen: "Mortarmen have been absolved of night-watch and all stonecutting since the time of Charles Martel, as men have understood from father to son." To be exempt from night-watch was an important privilege. It is certainly not logical that those who simply made mortar needed at least six years of apprenticeship or that they were exempt from night-watch, a rarely accorded favor. A careful distinction must be made between the men who worked with hard stone and the simple laborers who made mortar from that same stone.

Porters, cementers, mortarmen, and stonecutters were only one part of the family of stoneworkers; plasterers, plaster mixers, and masons made up the other part. The statutes of Étienne Boileau confirm this: "The cementer and the plasterer are of the same status and the same lodge of masons in all respects." The mason was above all else a stone layer. The English word explains this act of placing or setting stones, calling it "setting" or "laying." The English words that designate various specialized workers are quite interesting since they reveal the origin of the word "freemason" and give an insight into how "operative" freemasonry (which preceded the contemporary "speculative" freemansonry – composed of men not masons by profession: a social fraternal organization) was born and developed. We will return again to this very controversial question.

In the Cathedral of Bourges one window was donated by the masons and another by the stonecutters. Numerous manuscript illuminations depict masons at work. Most often they are represented working on walls with their tools: the trowel, level, and plumbline. At the foot of the walls cementers are shown mixing, and laborers carrying it or stones up to the masons.

Mason's names disappeared from the accounts in the winter since freezing weather put a stop to all stone laying. Before leaving the job, masons took great care to cover the upper part of the wall with straw or dung to protect the stones and joints from winter rains. Some of the masons more skilled at stonecutting remained in the shop or lodge at the foot of the walls. Others went to work in the quarries, and, finally, there were those who, being married, rejoined their wives and worked on their small farms during the winter. They rented their used wagons to the chapter to transport stone to the shop from the quarries. If a mason's annual wages were less than those of the stonecutters who were hired to work the year round, their daily wages were about the same. In the accounts of the Monastery of the Brothers of St. Augustine in Paris, both the masons and the stonecutters made at least twenty-two deniers per day:

> To 3 stonecutters, 5 days each: 27 sous 6 deniers
> (This would be 22 deniers per day.)
> To Regnaut de Senlis and Jehan de Meudon, masons, 4 days each at 22 deniers per day: 15 sous 4 deniers

This latter is an example of one of the frequent errors in calculation mentioned above. The sum should have been 14 sous 8 deniers, not 15 sous 4 deniers.

Masons enjoyed certain advantages. For example, the workshop foreman furnished them with gloves to protect their hands from lime burns, and they were given certain gratuities when a job was completed or when a keystone was put into place. Some of the more fortunate masons listed in the registry of stonecutters – for example, Gefroi and Symon de Baine, who were paid respectively 1 livre 4 sous and 2 livres 8 sous – could have been contractors capable of directing small workshops by contract.

The 104 masons mentioned in the roll of 1292, several of whom undoubtedly worked in the workshop at Notre-Dame de Paris, lived far from one another, scattered all over the city of Paris. Renaud the mason and Jehan Pasquier lived with the "little people," "beyond the Porte Saint-Honoré and the parish of Saint-Germain l'Auxerrois." Gautier the mason, Simon, Lorenz, and Tibaut lived in the Rue du Pilori right at the abbey. Pierre the mason lived in the Rue de la Boucherie.

One of the leading figures of the cathedral crusade was the quarryman, although he is often overlooked. He did not work at the shop, and he seems to have lived outside the community. Very few authors mention him. The first Étienne Boileau, failed to mention him in his statutes. Yet the quarryman left his youth and his health in the quarries. His was a life of pain, for he had to work under the most adverse conditions. He suffered from the dampness of many quarries and was frequently overcome by poisonous air in underground cuttings. He was poorly paid, hardly receiving more than a common laborer. In the Paris tax

register, the quarryman Guillaume, Pierre, Renaut, and Jehan were among the "little people" who paid only twelve deniers.

It was in the quarry that medieval man came to know stone, for it was there that he served his apprenticeship. No antique tradition had survived to teach him the qualities and faults of this primary material. He had to teach himself how to reckon bed or vein heights and compute their worth and, in general, he had to teach himself a feeling for stone.

The function of the quarryman in the first phase of each new project was singularly important. He had to extract thousands of cubic yards of stone required for foundations, and his work often began even before the workshop was established. When Edward I of England founded that country's last Cistercian Abbey at Vale Royal in Cheshire in 1277 at the crown's expense, the master of the works, Walter of Hereford, sent laborers into the quarry before actually opening the workshop.

They worked in groups of eight, each group under the command of a master quarryman. In a period of three years, from 1278 to 1281, exactly 35,448 cartloads of stone were transported from the quarry to the workshop about five miles away. Estimating roughly that each cartload of stone weighed a ton, 35,000 tons of stone must have been quarried. This means a cart would have left the quarry every fifteen minutes of a working day!

Knoop and Jones, two English historians who have scrupulously analyzed the accounts of these three years, have shown that while only five to ten per cent of the masons and stonecutters were recruited from the region, eighty-five per cent of the quarrymen were of local origin.

Master quarrymen such as Robert de Inis, Paul de Alueton or Richard Louekin received a salary twice as high as that of other quarrymen. This is given in terms of percentage to avoid misleading comparisons: English sous and deniers did not have the same value as the Parisian. Master quarrymen were generally paid for each stone extracted. Examining the account of the fabric at Autun, we see that Robert Clavel paid Master Chevillard, a master quarryman, so much for each stone quarried in proportion to its size. Thus Master Chevillard received

82

10 livres for a thousand stones, 2 livres 9 sous 6 deniers for 150 stones, and 4 livres for 200 stones. This means that he earned about 2 deniers for each stone of the first size, 4 deniers for each of the second size, and 5 for each of the third.

Certain individuals listed in the accounts as "quarrymen" were actually businessmen who rented or bought quarries which they exploited. These were men with a special standing. In the roll of 1292, Asce the quarryman paid 6 livres in taxes, 120 times more than quarrymen Guillaume, Pierre, or Jean. Asce obviously was not a laborer but a quarry owner. So also were Thibaut des Halles and Hugon, who were listed in the accounts of the Brothers of St. Augustine as "quarrymen": "To Hugon, quarryman of Notre-Dame des Champs, for large foundation stones ... 6 livres."

The cost of transporting stones in the Middle Ages was so high that it was essential to dress them at the quarry. It has been calculated that transporting a load of stone from the quarry to a workshop about twelve miles distant cost as much as to buy the stones in the quarry. Consequently, the workshop foreman often sent stonecutters to work at the quarry with given specifications. Measurements were generally given in terms of toises, feet, and inches. *

The Middle Ages sought to standardize stone measurements. In 1264 the city of Douai issued a legal publication specifying that all *carreaux* – blocks of stone shaped in parallelepipeds – coming into the city must have six by eight inches of facing (facing is the side of a stone visible in a wall) and eight inches of bed (in this case bed indicating the depth of the stone). This block was a stone that served as a header, the one with its small end exposed in the surface of a wall.

All the stones used in building the choir of the Augustinian monastery in Paris must have had the same dimensions since each one cost 2 deniers 8. All stonecutters who cut stones to measure, making allowances for bed height and thickness, were paid the same thing: "For cutting 128 measured stones and four feet of pavingstone, by the piece ... 64 sous. For cutting 112

* 6 feet = 1 toise.

measured stones and half a pavingstone, by the piece . . . 56 sous 9 deniers." The worker was here paid 6 deniers per toise.

On the other hand, stonecutters were sometimes paid by the day or the week, although no one knows exactly why some workers were paid by the job and others by the day. However, it seems probable that when an unknown worker presented himself to the foreman to be hired, he was hired by the job so that his skill and his work could be tested. After proving his professional capabilities, he could then be paid by the day. Needless to say, laborers preferred this second system of payment.

From numerous observations on masons' marks * incised on cathedrals, monasteries, fortified châteaux, and city fortification walls in various provinces in France, the following hypothesis can be drawn concerning piecework. It seems to have been a mode of payment more frequent in the twelfth century than in the thirteenth; more widespread in Alsace, south of the Loire, and particularly in Provence, than in the north; more usual in little workshops such as that of the Brothers of St. Augustine than in the large workshops such as at Chartres or Amiens where it seems practically nonexistent. Commandeered workers were generally paid by the piece. The walls of Aigues-Mortes are literally covered with the marks of pieceworkers; and we know that in 1244 it was necessary to requisition workers from Alès to force them to work at Aigues-Mortes "under penalty of their persons and their goods." The same was also true at the fortified Château de Coucy, raised so rapidly in the thirteenth century, and built by common laborers commandeered by the powerful lord of Coucy. On these walls over sixty different masons' marks have been found.

What exactly is a mason's mark? Each stonecutter had to have a distinctive sign which he could engrave on any one of the faces of the cut stone when he was being paid by the piece to permit the workshop foreman to check on the quality of his work and at the end of the week to total up the number of stones he had cut and pay him accordingly. There is a great variety of signs. There are

---

* These marks were not made only by masons. The designation is a general one for all pieceworkers' marks. (Trans. note.)

geometrical figures such as triangles or pentagons, tools such as pickaxes or hammers, crosses, letters of the alphabet representing perhaps the first letter in the worker's name. Occasionally a worker engraved the first three letters of his name and, rarely, even his whole name. In the eleventh and twelfth centuries these signs were cut very roughly but in the thirteenth they were cut much more carefully. Fathers handed down their marks to their sons. While their fathers were still alive, sons had to make a distinction between their identical marks. For example, if a father's mark was a cross (+), his son might use a cross with an additional mark (+'). Little by little these marks acquired a sentimental value, and certain of those found on the nave piers at Notre-Dame de Paris, for example, or on the transept piers at Chartres were engraved by stonecutters engaged by the day or by the week simply as expressions of personal pride. Eventually masons' marks developed into types of signatures. In the fifteenth century an architect such as Alexandre de Berneval placed a five-pointed star after his name.

Since numerous masons' marks have been found in monasteries it is clear that the orders employed outside help in building their abbeys. They have been found at Sylvacane, at Senanque on the pillars of the nave, at Montmajour, at Fontenay in the Côte-d'Or, on the exterior wall at the famous Benedictine church in Issoire.

Many of these signs were cut on the engaged face of the stone and were not discovered until the walls were destroyed. Marks engraved on church interiors were not visible because the walls were covered with paintings. The masons who laid these stones cared nothing about the marks and occasionally they are found opposite the facing. By systematically studying the marks of a given region, one can trace workers, in exceptional cases, from one workshop to another.

Certain masons' marks were the work of quarrymen. It was necessary to identify the source of stone coming from two quarries into one workshop: this was very important to the future solidity of the construction because each wall had to be built of stones from the same source to insure that it would settle evenly. Quarry marks also insured that later repairs would be made with

Stonecutters' marks taken from Strasbourg Cathedral

the correct stone. The Romans also seem to have used this method of marking since quarry marks are found on stones in their buildings.

One must not confuse masons' and quarrymen's marks with "position marks." When it was necessary to assemble a number of stones the dresser gave precise instructions to the stonecutters, that they cut in such and such a manner the different blocks for future assembly. This being done, masons could, when the time came, accurately fit these stones together before cementing them. The Romans had previously employed this method of construction, and position marks are found engraved on the stones of the Pont du Gard, for example. The inscriptions indicate the positions of the blocks in the construction (*fronte dextra, fronte sinistra*). One can read on the fourth arch of the second tier: FR.S.II FR.S.III FR.S.IIII FR.D.V.. In the twentieth century position marks are still used in constructing large stone buildings.

Position marks are not generally apparent in medieval construction until the stone sections have been dismantled; then it is seen that in arches, for example, stones which were to be adjoining had matching marks incised in the faces to be joined. This permitted pieces to be put up in the same order that they were cut. When several arches had the same profile, each arch had a particular mark to differentiate it from the others. One of the piers in the smithy of Fontenay Abbey has exposed position marks.

Position marks were also used to assure that the placement of statues was not confused. The sculptures symbolizing months of the year had been inverted at Notre-Dame de Paris. The master of the workshop at Reims did not want to suffer a similar misadventure with his three thousand statues, so he conceived a system of incised annotations to show a mason exactly where to place each statue assigned to him. The position marks indicated which façade of the cathedral and which portal was to contain a given statue and its position in that portal.

Reims: position marks

FREEMASONS AND SCULPTORS

When Walter of Hereford sent laborers to the quarry at Vale Royal, he had his carpenters build one lodge of fourteen hundred boards to accommodate the stone-cutters. The following year he built a smaller lodge of one thousand boards. Whether the stonecutters were paid by the piece or by the week, their lives centered in or around the lodge. In the morning they went to get their tools, they had lunch there, and in very hot weather they took siestas there. There were always one or more lodges at the workshop, and they can be seen located at the foot of buildings under construction in manuscript illuminations.

The lodges not only gave workers a place in which to eat and rest, but they provided a place in which stone-cutters could work in bad weather. For this reason these lodges were very important during the winter months. Stonecutters stayed in the lodges then and, sheltered from the elements, prepared work for the masons who would return to the shop only with the coming of good weather. Yet nights were not spent in the lodges. In the cathedral cities, workers were housed in inns or in private homes. Due to the isolation of abbeys, wood dormitories were erected for workers engaged in monastic construction programs.

The lodge became, in addition to being a place for work and rest, a place in which problems of interest to all could be discussed. In a way it was a club, and this was the early beginning of masonic lodges in the modern sense. The discussions carried on there could become

91

Van Eyck's Saint Barbara. *At the foot of the edifice, the stonecutters' lodge*

very heated. A text preserved in the Cartulary of Notre-Dame de Paris cites an incident that happened in that cathedral's lodge on Assumption Eve. It must have been rather serious since reference to it was made in 1283 concerning a battle for control between the chapter and the bishop of Paris. And the chapter must have used armed intervention to control the situation. Little by little, chapters came to control lodge life, the earliest known rule being that handed down by the chapter of York in 1352.

Masons and stonecutters were part of an essentially floating working force, with many factors contributing to their migration from workshop to workshop and from country to country. Younger masons aspired to new horizons, to learn new customs and different tech-

A contemporary Masonic Lodge: the Volney lodge at Laval

niques. Awed by their times, they wanted to see the incredibly audacious edifices that were springing up nearly everywhere in the Christian world. In a year's time they could expect to be hired successively at Mont-Saint-Michel, Mans, Paris, Reims, and Strasbourg. There were no borders and no passports in those days, and masons could cross the Rhine to the east to work at Cologne or over the Channel to the west to work at Canterbury. What pride and pleasure a laborer must have had in returning to his home town to describe the wonders he had seen! The villagers would recall that he had left home still almost a child to work in the nearby quarry. Inspired by faith, some masons accompanied the crusaders into Asia where they built the famous Krac of the knights and other strong forts to protect holy places. Still others went along with famous architects summoned to countries far across the sea, for example, the stonecutters who went with Étienne de Bonneuil when he sailed to Sweden to build the cathedral at Upsala. Bachelors were of course more attracted by the call to travel than married men. The latter were very careful not to go too far from their homes, in order to return at regular intervals.

Those who chose a wandering life did not all do so solely for the thrill of travel. Some quit one workshop to find another where the pay was higher. Often, too, workers took to the road to find new work not of their own free will but because the shop was closing, because the foreman, dissatisfied with their work, fired them without notice or pay, or because funds were exhausted and the shop closed while work was temporarily suspended.

On the other hand, conscription threw men onto the roads against their will and effected a major mobility among the builders, particularly in England where the king had the power to order county sheriffs to recruit twenty-five to forty men and send them to a castle workshop sometimes hundreds of miles away. French conscription did not cause such a migration of workers because no lord, not even the king, had the authority necessary to requisition laborers from such a great distance.

The life of these builders contrasted sharply with that of other laborers in the Middle Ages, who were for the most part sedentary workers living in the same place the year round. They traveled only exceptionally, and then not for business reasons. In the public interest and for the commercial prosperity of their cities, municipal councils in the thirteenth century became concerned about these stationary workers and succeeded in establishing, with the approval of the city's more important business-men, charters to organize the trades and to form what would someday become associations. Until the cities intervened, there was rarely any organization by laborers other than into charitable groups which have survived today as mutual aid societies.

Turning to the situation in England, where fortunately numerous charters such as those at York and Coventry are preserved, one notices the absence of documents concerning masons and stonecutters. This is explained by their predominantly migratory character, which allowed them to escape municipal control. Moreover, these men worked for the Church or noblemen, who had no interest in organizing guilds on their projects. The Church lacked interest because organized workers could band together disputing methods of employment and wages. Lords opposed organization because eventually workers would oppose the convenient conscription system.

The first English city to make an exception was London, where in the late fourteenth century traces of a professional organization of stonecutters and masons appeared. But London was then a city of fifty thousand people, five to ten times more populous than York or Coventry. There were necessarily more builders there than in a less important city, and they were consequently in a better position to organize themselves and to defend their right to do so. The very size of London assured its builders of constant employment and made them less dependent on their two traditional patrons, the Church and the nobility. There was a law concerning "masons, stonecutters, plasterers, and cementers" in Étienne Boileau's book for this same reason: Paris was a city of nearly two hundred thousand inhabitants, while Chartres and Amiens had only five or ten thousand. It was Boileau's forty-eighth entry that bore the royal seal, and as pointed out above, the king appointed his own master mason, Guillaume de Saint-Patu, to mastership over the guild in Paris. This of course facilitated finding workers for royal works.

The Latin terms that designated workers who cut stone in the Middle Ages do not generally permit a distinction to be made between those who simply quarried the stone and those who cut the vault stones, window tracery, and monumental portal sculpture. The sculptors were lost among the general mass of stonecutters. This is really rather extraordinary to us, because an enormous difference seems to exist between those who perform a seemingly mechanical task, such as cutting blocks of stone, and those who sculpt, *with their very soul,* the magnificent statues in the cathedrals. The truth is that for the great majority of men in the Middle Ages there was between a good *work* and a *masterpiece* only a difference of degree, not a difference of kind. The idea that there is an unbridgeable gulf between a worker and an artist (in the modern sense of the word) did not really occur until the Renaissance when it was expressed by intellectuals who judged, classified, and evaluated manual labor which was very foreign to them.

It was the Renaissance writers who, for the first time in history, extolled the personal merits of painters and sculptors, resulting in an excessive deification of both, the consequences of which are still felt. The Renaissance fabricated the notion of "the artist." The medieval thinker hardly ever expressed himself in his writings on actual questions of aesthetics, and when he did concern himself with what we call "art," it was in terms of theology or philosophy. Why? Did he more or less consciously hold manual labor in disdain and relegate both sculptor and mason to the same ill-favored category? Was he insensitive to the beauty of forms? Or was it because he intuitively perceived that a beautiful statue or a beautiful window were complete works in themselves, sufficient in themselves and thus requiring no comment? (In this connection it should be noted that the glorification of the "artist" since the Renaissance, even though

it would seem to be a promotion, has been nothing more than a placement of art under the guardianship of literature. Art henceforth was always to await its justification from literature.)

To avoid this problem of terminology, the word "artist" is deliberately not used here, since it adds nothing to the greatness of the cathedral builders and because its current meaning is essentially foreign to the spirit of the Middle Ages. Only in the dictionary of the French Academy of 1762 was "artist" mentioned in the sense that we now understand it.

In England, however, the terms that designated stone-cutters permit a certain distinction to be made between laborers who did the heavy work and those who executed the more refined work. This distinction is based on the characteristics of the stone worked. For example, those who worked the particularly hard stone found in Kent were known as "hard hewers." They were distinguished from "freestone masons" who worked the beautiful calcareous stone found in great abundance from Dorset to the Yorkshire coast and which was perfect for the delicate work of sculpture-carving. "Freestone masons" were also distinguished from "rough masons" who simply rough-hewed the stone.

The expression "freestone mason" was replaced after a while by the simplified "freemason," a word which evidently had to do with the quality of stone and not with any franchise which would have benefited builders. When honorary freemasonry was introduced into France from England about 1725, it was naturally translated as *franc-maçonnerie,* an expression unknown in the Middle Ages. On the other hand, it is known that in London in 1351 a *maître maçon de franche peer* was more or less the Anglo-French equivalent of two Latin expressions: *sculptores lapidum liberorum* (London, 1212) and *magister lathomus liberarum petrarum* (Oxford, 1391). The modern English and French translations of this second term would be: *a master mason of freestone* and *un maître tailleur de franche pierre.*

Application of the words *franc* or *franche* ("free") to stone in France has survived uninterruptedly to the present. The beautiful building-stone found in the region

Abbey church of Saint-Gilles: head of an Apostle (twelfth century)

about Paris has long been spoken of as "free liais," a term which is still applied to veins of excellent quality. When I visited the underground quarries of Paris, an engineer in charge of supervising the subterranean part of the capital showed me the inner side of a tunnel and told me, much to my surprise, that to designate veins of stone of the very best quality one would say "free veins."

Stone used for sculpture did not often have the same grain as that used for building the walls to which the statues were attached. A rapid glance at the *Portail Royal* at Chartres is sufficient to show that the stone of these famous statue-columns was not taken from the quarry at Berchères. And at Vézelay the capitals are not of the same stone used in buildings the rest of the church.

The frequent trips made by stonecutters from shop to shop, gave them the opportunity to examine stone from many quarries. It was made possible for some of them to work with the stone best suited to their capabilities, and others were able to have stone ordered from a specific quarry for a specific difficult job. The sculptors had a true love for material of high quality. Knowing the high cost of transportation at this time, one can only admire the intelligent understanding of those who bore the additional expense of these costly shipments of stone.

Studying the sculptor's position in medieval life and his role in the complex problem of the iconography of the time makes it clear that his position was constantly changing from the beginning of the eleventh century until well into the fourteenth. Any concern with the problem of creativity naturally raises the question of the sculptor's part in the choice and execution of these masterpieces. Due to the lack of texts, one is frequently reduced to more or less accurate hypotheses on the subject. But, so far as possible we must abstain from our modern way of thinking. The danger of using the word "artist" to describe or recall these creators of the past has already been pointed out.

One way of arriving at a better understanding of the creators of a given period is to relocate them in the framework of the history of oral, literary, or visual techniques of expression according to their historical situation. In

"Stone for sculptures has a different grain from stone for walls" (Chartres: Royal Portal)

this case it is the visual. Paleolithic man expressed himself by shaping bone objects or by means of wall paintings such as those at Lascaux; the Greeks of the fifth century B.C. by painting of terra cotta vases or marble sculpture such as that of the Parthenon; the Byzantines by ivory work or great mosaics such as those at the Hagia Sophia; the Italian Renaissance by bronze sculpture or easel-painting; the United States by movies or television. These techniques of expression provide a partial insight into the religious thought and ethics of the society. But tech-

99

niques of expression are in a state of perpetual evolution, one in connection with the others, susceptible to transformations of thought and material changes in the communities where they appear. Some for a time reach a level which we consider a great means of expression, whereas others lose their privileged status to become secondary or forgotten means of expression.

Theologians expressed the medieval thought of the tenth and eleventh centuries in frescoes, gold work, and miniatures, which were the primary means of expression at that time, but not in sculpture. In the course of the eleventh century when stonecutters, thanks to a better understanding of their material, began to carve little representational scenes, they doubtless did so freely and without ecclesiastical supervision. Their timid, gauche attempts received little attention, but their ceaseless efforts and progress finally attracted monastic attention by the end of the eleventh century to this new technique, in the western Christian world. Monks made personal contracts with these sculptors and gave them themes to execute. Thus was born in southwest France and Burgundy the monumental sculpture that first appeared in the Cluniac priories of Moissac, Toulouse, Autun, and Vézelay. Society was then bathed in a religious atmosphere: from his youth on the stonecutter was in daily contact, at home as well as in the Church, with the scenes that served as subjects for his creations. There was something of a universally common inspiration which explains how a given subject retained its identity almost perfectly in regions far distant from one another.

Monumental sculpture rapidly developed and became a major means of expression from the twelfth century on. From the middle of the century stained glass in its turn gained considerable importance at the expense of frescoes, as window areas increased and wall surfaces diminished. In the thirteenth century fresco-painting became a lost means of expression.

Within what limits did the sculptor's freedom evolve? In the first place, it must be made clear that in an "ascendant" period there can be no creators who are misunderstood or in opposition to those who commission work. There can be only divergent opinions on details.

It is certainly wrong to think that the Lascaux painters made their point of view prevail over that of the magicians who were the theologians of the time. The sculptors of the Parthenon were able to discuss form with the priests within certain limits, but no more. This submission of creator to the directives of magician or priest is natural to creation. It was a principle or a tradition so self-evident that only rarely have societies had occasion to state it in writing. A famous exception to this rule was that document compiled by the Church Fathers at the Second Council of Nicaea in 787. They were faced with the necessity of clarifying what, until the extraordinarily bitter iconoclastic controversy broke out, had long been clear to the Catholic Church. It was stated that

> the composition of religious images is not left to the inspiration of artists; it exemplifies those principles established by the Catholic Church and religious tradition. Art pertains only to paintings, its composition to the Fathers.

It would be impossible to be more explicit. In removing the *Christ* from the choir of the famous church of Assy in Haute-Savoie, the Church was only complying with the principles established at the Council of Nicaea twelve centuries earlier. One might ask if the Nicene text should not be placed in capital letters at the entrance to exhibitions of sacred art, and if everyone desiring to work for the Church should not be required to memorize it.

Becoming a sculptor, the stonecutter rose to the world of the spirit. He was closer to the theologians and learned more through this contact; he had the wonderful opportunity to thumb through precious manuscripts in abbeys; he learned to look, observe, think. His intellectual horizon was expanding, which permitted him to participate spiritually as well as physically in his creations. Thanks to the manuscript minatures leafed through and admired in various abbeys, the sculptor could humbly suggest slight variations in the subjects proposed by the Fathers. Since the sculptor and the theologian worked toward the same goal, the sculptor could consider himself free, for in this association he did not submit to any constraint. In this sense it could be said that the difference between the artist of today and the medieval sculptor is that the latter was not an individualist since he did not claim the rights of personal inspiration. However, a legitimate pride did overcome the spirit of these workers with humble backgrounds, and sculptors did not hesitate, especially in the twelfth century, to sign their works. Gislebert signed the famous tympanum of Autun: *"Gislebertus fecit hoc opus."* Giraud signed the portal of Saint-Ursin in Bourges; Umbert, a capital of the porch at Saint-Benoît-sur-Loire; Rettibitus, a capital of Notre-Dame du Port in Clermont.

Sculptors were not the only workers who signed their creations. The mason Durandus signed one of the vault keystones at Rouen Cathedral about 1233 with *"Durandus me fecit."* And in the same cathedral, the glassmaker Clément de Chartres signed his window. This Latin term *me fecit* must be used carefully, remembering that it

Autun: the tympanum

could concern the person who ordered or paid for the work as well as its actual creator. Yet it is obviously incorrect to insist on the absolute anonymity of the cathedral builders. Not all medieval sculpture is signed, but then neither is all that at Versailles, and no one has ever considered the sculptors of the seventeenth century anonymous.

The sculptor often worked on a block of stone already in place in the building. This was true, for example, with the capitals at Vézelay. The sculpture executed on the façade of Saint-Ferdinand des Termes in Paris' 17th Arrondissement in 1957 was worked like many twelfth-century pieces, right on the wall. The sculpture thus becomes an integral part of the building. Statue-columns of the twelfth century, such as those of the *Portail Royal* at Chartres, show this close collaboration between sculptor and architect, a magnificent harmony that unhappily lasted only a short time. The sculptor, perhaps having lost a little of his former humility, wanted to make his work independent, so he detached his sculpture from the column. From that time forth he worked his block of stone in the lodge, away from the church. He is seen working in this way in the thirteenth century in a stained glass window that he, together with the other stonecutters, offered to Our Lady of Chartres.

Intoxicated by his freedom and his extraordinary success in the spiritual and physical order of things, he dreamed only of putting sculpture everywhere. He wanted literally to cover churches with his creations and he suffocated them. Compositions became confused. Some of the twelve hundred sculptures at Notre-Dame de Paris were misplaced on the building. At Reims it was necessary to number the cathedral's three thousand sculptures in much the same way that prefabricated parts are numbered today. At Tournai sculptors established themselves and produced works to order. In 1272 the abbot of Cambron bargained over prices with two sculptors to cut and ship cut-to-specification window mullions to Brussels.

Having broken with the architect, the sculptor next dissociated himself from the theologian. Did he already consider himself better than the mortals around him?

Was this the dawn of the Renaissance? He constantly had to be brought back into line. The period of Christian expansion was over. In 1306 the sculptor Tideman executed a Christ for a London church which did not conform to the accepted conventions. The bishop actively intervened, had the Christ removed, and ordered Tideman to return his fee.

Such freedom for the sculptor from all tradition, something that would have been impossible a century earlier, coincided with a general weakening of the Faith. The powerful and rich who previously had given their riches to the cathedral now devoted their fortunes to increasing their own comfort and satisfying their taste for life. They built private chapels and city houses. Activity in the great workshops ground to a halt as the better sculptors and builders were hired away and hired to build and ornament the mansions and chapels of the nobility. The situation was similar to that in Athens in the fifth and fourth centuries B.C.: the progressive era for Athens ended with the Peloponnesian Wars. Throughout the fifth century sculptors worked on such projects as the Parthenon, but Athens was ruined in the fourth century and rich individuals hired sculptors – Praxiteles, for example – to appease their egotistic appetite for beauty.

But the French sculptor of the fourteenth century for a long time could not profit from working for private individuals because the Hundred Years' War, beginning in 1337, disrupted both his life and tranquility. It ended prosperity and travel for the sculptor. National revenue fell sharply. Misery and poverty were felt everywhere, and plagues, famine, and battle all but decimated the population. Rare indeed were the privileged who could still engage sculptors. Life was of and for the war, a situation in which sculpture was only a luxury. Workshops either closed or slowed down, most sculptors were impressed into military service and then forced to build military structures such as prisons and fortified castles. Needless to say, delicate skill was not a primary concern. Local stone was used since it was impossible to haul better stone from great distances during the war. With the impossibility of travel, new generations of workers forgot where the famous quarries which had provided stone for monumental sculpture were located. It is difficult to recognize in these sculptors – compelled as they were to carve stone cannonballs – the descendants of those who built Chartres and Mont-Saint-Michel.

When the Hundred Years' War ended in the mid-fifteenth century, and stonecutters once again began to sculpt, they could not return to the great tradition of the cathedral crusade regardless of their efforts. The world had changed, and in its turn stone sculpture had ceased to be a living means of expression.

Ypres

THE ARCHITECTS

In 1955 the Bibliothèque Nationale in Paris included in its great exhibition of French illuminated manuscripts from the thirteenth to the sixteenth century the *Sketchbook* of Villard de Honnecourt, the thirteenth-century architect from Honnecourt, a small village in Picardy between Cambrai and Vaucelles. This extraordinary document from the hand of a true cathedral builder contains thirty-three parchment leaves inscribed both recto and verso and is quite familiar to historians. The nineteenth-century architect Lassus published it in a facsimile edition accompanied by a detailed commentary. Fortunately this edition is found in all major libraries and permits anyone interested in the Middle Ages and its architecture to study Villard's plans profitably without having to consult the original in the Bibliothèque Nationale. The latest editor and commentator of the document was Hahnloser, who clarified certain obscure points in 1935. Unhappily, this edition was published in German in Vienna and has not yet been translated into French or English. *

This truly encyclopedic thirteenth-century text is of an unparalleled richness. Several of the plans included in the manuscript are generally known by the public, but not all. Normally, it seems satisfactory to reproduce only Villard's essays on triangulation although the document's major interest is its revelation of the universal curiosity of the thirteenth-century architect. It was noted above

* The most recent edition in America is that by Theodore Bowie, *The Sketchbook of Villard de Honnecourt*, Bloomington, Indiana, 1959.

Life of Saint Offar *(thirteenth century)*

that the synthesizing spirit which characterized the Middle Ages is unlike the contemporary analytical mind with its excessive specialization.

Since World War II young architects – probably due to Le Corbusier's influence – have, in a sense, learned to think of achitecture in its totality. The contemporary urbanist is very close to Villard. He studies all the problems of his time. Architects have too long been theorists interested only in the aesthetics of architecture; but now the human side of urbanism again brings together the human considerations of a Villard de Honnecourt. Despite everything, the eighteenth-century architect had an advantage over his twentieth-century colleague: more or less trained in the workshop, he knew how to operate it without outside intervention from a contractor.

Villard introduces himself in his document in this way:

> Villard de Honnecourt greets you and begs all who will use the devices found in this book to pray for his soul and remember him. For in this book will be found sound advice on the virtues of masonry and the uses of carpentry. You will also find strong help in drawing figures according to the lessons taught by the art of geometry. *

Villard's interest in carpentry is worth noting. An architect of his time had to have a profound knowledge of the trade of carpentry because the master carpenter was no less important than the master mason or the master stonecutter. Under Philippe le Bel, for example, the royal master carpenter and the royal master mason received identical salaries and benefits. Whether they were at the palace or not, they received 4 sous a day and a bonus of 100 sous paid on All Saints' Day, and in addition to this they were allowed to eat at the palace and each was provided with two horses shod at the palace forge.

Part of the Villard manuscript is unfortunately missing, and it is precisely that part concerning carpentry. This is a great loss because with it much more knowledge of

---

* All English translation of Villard de Honnecourt's work from Theodore Bowie, *The Sketchbook of Villard de Honnecourt*, Bloomington, Indiana University Press, 1959.

108

Life of Saint Denis *(fourteenth century)*

the generally little known world of wood would be available.

Quicherat observed that the subjects contained in the manuscript can be classified as follows: (1) mechanics, (2) practical geometry and trigonometry, (3) carpentry, (4) architectural design, (5) ornamental design, (6) figure designs, (7) furniture designs, and (8) subjects foreign to the special knowledge of architects and designers.

Originally this manuscript was a true sketchbook. Villard jotted down those things which interested him so he could draw on them later for his own designs. Hahnloser observed that not all the entries are by the same hand, and he concluded that the notes, which were private at the beginning, eventually became the property of the whole workshop. When Villard died the *Sketchbook* must have been passed on to other architects who added designs and comments to it.

We think that in a period of growth there can be no

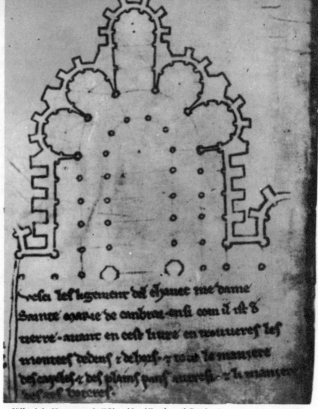

Villard de Honnecourt's "Sketchbook": plan of Cambrai

misunderstood creators, that in such a period the saying, "a prophet is without honor in his own country," does not hold true. Villard worked in the same region where he was born. He may have rebuilt the Cathedral of Cambrai near Honnecourt, of which he gives a plan of the choir:

> This is the plan of the choir of Our Lady of Cambrai as it is now rising from the ground. Earlier in this book you will find the inner and outer elevations, as well as the arrangement of the chapels, the walls, and the flying buttresses. [8]

This cathedral was destroyed in the early nineteenth century but an extraordinary piece of luck has preserved a photograph of an old wax relief map of the city of Cambrai, which shows the choir constructed in Villard's time (and perhaps by him). This relief map was part of a secret collection, created at the command of Louis XIV, which represented cities of strategic importance and their immediate surroundings. These models were evidently withheld from the curiosity of the public and foreign diplomats; they were still made in the eighteenth century and even during part of the nineteenth. No longer of any military value, they now constitute the basis of the very interesting museum of relief maps temporarily located in the attic of the Hôtel des Invalides in Paris. When Paris was occupied in 1815 following Napoleon's defeat, the Germans seized the opportunity to send certain of them to Berlin, one being that of Cambrai and its cathedral. Placed in the Berlin Arsenal, it was unwittingly destroyed during the bombing and fire in the German capital in 1944. Thus the photograph of the relief is all that now shows this thirteenth-century cathedral.

Like other stonecutters and architects of his day, Villard de Honnecourt traveled a great deal, and thanks to his *Sketchbook,* we can follow some of his pilgrimages. He visited Reims where he drew elevations of the cathedral; Chartres, where he copied the west façade rose and the labyrinth (which he traced in a reverse direction); Meaux; and Laon, where he very judiciously admired the cathedral's famous towers. He took great care in drawing the oxen which are still curiously placed in the corners of the towers. He went to Switzerland; to Lausanne for example, where he drew one of the cathedral's rose windows. But he went even farther, crossing Germany to go to Hungary. He tells about it himself: "This is one of the windows of Reims, in the area of the nave, as it stands between two pillars. I had been invited to go to Hungary when I drew this, which is why I liked it all the more." While in Hungary it is possible that he built the cathedral dedicated to Saint Elizabeth at Marburg.

During these numerous trips Villard sketched, here and there, many things that interested him. He observed nature and animals, he drew insects – a grasshopper, a

111

dragonfly, a bee, a snail; birds, wild animals – a hare and a wild boar; and animals – a cat, a dog, horses. He also drew animals that he saw in menageries – lion cubs, a lion, a bear; and an imaginary animal – the dragon. These designs were to serve as models for him or for the sculptors who worked under him. For the same reason he drew numerous figures, taking great care with drapery – a Christ on the cross with the figures of St. John and the Virgin, a descent from the cross (a scene rarely drawn at that time), a Virgin and Child, and the Twelve Apostles. In addition to these holy people he drew two men shooting dice (probably masons playing on a gauging board) and two wrestlers. He also drew nudes, the designs for some of which were certainly inspired by antiquity, and he reproduced certain antique fragments. Roman monuments were then much more numerous than now and the contact between the Middle Ages and antiquity rather close. With very few exceptions most Latin works were known to scholars in the Middle Ages, but they did not have the sometimes devoted and often systematic admiration of the Renaissance for everything concerning antiquity.

As noted above, some of the most frequently reproduced Villard drawings are those related to his essays on triangulation. But too much importance need not be attached to this expedient method of design since it was only a useful scheme. Villard was interested in those little inventions of which the Middle Ages seems to have been so fond and which Americans now call "gadgets." He was especially interested in mechanical contraptions, even for the Church: "How to make the eagle face the Deacon while the Gospel is being read." Following this he designed and described a hand-warmer intended for a bishop:

> If you wish to make a hand-warmer, you must first make a kind of brass apple with two fitting halves. Inside this brass apple, there must be six brass rings, each with two pivots, and in the middle there must be a little brazier with two pivots. The pivots must be alternated in such a way that the brazier always remains upright, for each ring bears the pivots of the others. If

112

Ancient technique...

you follow the instructions and the drawing, the coals will never drop out, no matter which way the brazier is turned. A bishop may freely use this device at High Mass; his hands will not get cold as long as the fire lasts. That is all there is to it.

This system was later adopted to keep mariners' compasses horizontally level and barometers vertical. Villard explained in detail the operation of a hydraulic toy, then very much the rage, and a gully-hole, which is a machine constructed on the principle of a siphon. On another page, by means of the movement of a clock which is schematically indicated, we learn "how to make an angel keep pointing his finger toward the sun."

114

...and medieval technique

Villard was not only interested in these "gadgets," however. He was an avid engineer interested in serious problems and inventions such as leverage machines. He invented a screw combined with a lever, and he wrote "how to make the most powerful engine for lifting weights."

Medieval miniatures show workers operating windlasses and hand-winches which seem to be like those used by the Romans. It is known that the system of the inclined plane, used by the Egyptians to build the pyramids, was practically never used to lift stones in cathedral construction, evidently prohibited by houses surrounding the churches.

Large treadwheels in which one or two men walked

much like squirrels were used to hoist materials up for construction. The physical exertion required to operate these treadwheels and gears was not excessive. Several of these great wheels can still be seen: there is one at Mont-Saint-Michel, one at Bourges over the vaults, and over the vaults of various Alsatian churches. They were left in place when the workshops closed to facilitate hoisting material needed later to repair vault webs, roofs, etc.

It was the master carpenters who must have been charged with inventing and constructing these lifting devices. Because they were so costly to make, they were not disassembled when the workshop closed and the chapter could rent them when necessary.

Villard de Honnecourt occupied himself solving such difficult problems as how to cut timber under water. In the *Sketchbook* he drew a machine that he believed would do this, and he wrote under the drawing: "By this means, one can cut off the tops of piles under water, so as to set a pier on them." And he was careful to indicate in the drawing that it was necessary to place a level and a plumb-bob along the pile to guarantee the structure's verticality.

Like many others since, he tried to build a perpetual-motion machine which would free man from slavery to manual labor. Under the drawing of it he wrote: "Often have experts striven to make a wheel turn of its own accord. Here is a way to do it with an uneven number of mallets and with quicksilver." He was of course mistaken about the perpetual character of his machine, but he did invent a semi-automatic machine to replace human power in sawing wood efficiently: "How to make a saw operate itself." This device was actually operated by hydraulic power, very much in use in the Middle Ages.

And everywhere Villard's interest in geometry is obvious:

> Here begins the method of drawing as taught by the art of geometry, to facilitate working. . . . On these four pages are figures of the art of geometry, but to understand them one must be careful to learn the peculiar use of each. . . . All these devices are extracted from geometry.

116

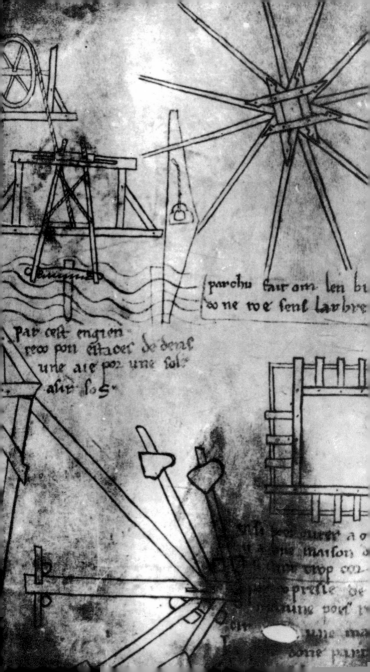

parchu fair om len bi
co ne roe fent larbre

par cest engien
recor pon eftacer de deuf
une aie por une foif
aiir fos

enli por ouirer a o
ene maifon o
mu crop cor
oprefle de
une poi
une ma
cone pur

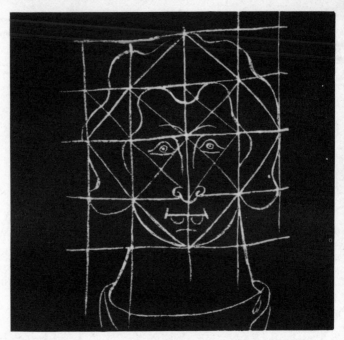

From Villard de Honnecourt's "Sketchbook"

Using geometry, one can measure the height of a building or the width of a river: "How to measure the height of a tower." How to measure the width of a watercourse without crossing it." "How to make two vessels so that one holds twice as much as the other."

Lassus investigated the extent of Villard's grasp of geometry, and he observed that

finding the center of a circle after locating three points on its circumference and proving a square indicate a knowledge of the properties of a circle and perpendiculars. Measuring the distance from one point to another or the height of a tower without being near either is based on equilateral triangles with certain conditions known. The problem of one vase having twice the capacity of another is based on the measure of a circle and the square of the hypotenuse. The drawings of a cloister presuppose a knowledge of the properties of the diagonals of a rectangle.

Villard offered means by which stonecutters could accurately outline a stone's dimensions: "How to cut an oblique voussoir." "How to cut the springing-stone of an arch." "How to make regular pendants: Place them upside down."

It is interesting to ask where Villard and the other architects of his time acquired their knowledge of geometry, a science which was unknown to the eleventh century. An examination of the correspondence exchanged about 1025 between the scholars Ragimbold de Cologne and Radolf de Liège, two intellectuals of the time, strikingly reveals the level of knowledge of geometry in the eleventh century and proves that nearly every Greek text had been lost during the course of the high Middle Ages. Their correspondence shows that the authors were incapable of finding by themselves anything that could be called geometric science. The historian Paul Tannery has written that "an analysis of these letters reduces itself to proving their ignorance." Ragimbold and Radolf discussed the definition of the exterior angle of a triangle (a term they found in one of the rare works of antiquity in their possession) without arriving at any agreement about it. Nor could either set up a true demonstration of the theorem concerning the equality of two right angles to the sum of the angles of a triangle. Several years later Francon de Liège was still vainly seeking the solution to this problem, and we know that other scholars – Wazron, Razegan, and Adelman – also tried this proof. So several generations were uselessly spent on a relatively simple problem without ever finding an answer.

If it can be proved that the intellectuals of the Middle Ages did not reinvent geometry and that Greek texts had almost entirely disappeared from western Europe, where did men such as Villard de Honnecourt obtain their information? Part doubtless came by direct transmission from Roman ruins and through study of the work of Vitruvius, a Roman architect of the first century B.C. whose manuscripts were copied throughout the high

Middle Ages. But above all, it seems certain that architects drew their vast knowledge from Arabic scholarship. During the course of the ninth and tenth centuries Moslem scholars had translated a great part of the scientific works of classical antiquity into Arabic, notably the works of Aristotle, Plato, Euclid, and Ptolemy. The Arabs, ordering in a magnificent synthesis the knowledge obtained from classical antiquity and from India, assimilated arithmetical knowledge, developed chemistry and algebra, and for all practical purposes invented trigonometry. This vast culture was taught in Arabic universities in Spain in the eleventh and twelfth centuries to Moslem as well as to Christian and Jewish students. Raymond, Archbishop of Toledo from 1126 to 1151, established a school of translators to translate from Arabic into Latin texts of both Greek and Arabic authors. It was thus that Adélard of Bath translated the complete works of Euclid at a time when western Europe still knew only the enunciation of several of his theorems. In 1145 Robert of Chester translater the algebraic work of Al-Khawarizmi. This date marks the appearance of algebra into Europe. Gérard of Cremona translated Ptolemy's *Almagest* and Al-Zarqali's works on trigonometry, which demonstrate the uses of signs and tangents. Plato's *Timaeus, Meno,* and *Phaedo* were also translated.

By the middle of the twelfth century Greek and Arabic scientific culture was accessible to western European scholars. The Arabic element in the foundation of our civilization is often underestimated, although it permitted the full flowering of the Middle Ages. Without this formidable basis the Renaissance would have developed slowly and painfully. And we in the twentieth century would perhaps be only at the scientific and technical level of the last century. The United States would doubtless still be in the horse and buggy era.

In the schools (of Chartres and Paris) such men as Villard or his twelfth-century predecessors might have gained knowledge of this scientific culture, as well as by studying Latin and Picard manuscripts. At the school of Chartres in the mid-twelfth century one could follow the courses of Thierry de Chartres and Guillaume de Conches, both of whom were familiar with Aristotle's

120

theories of physics. Also, certain scientific works written in Latin were in turn translated into the Romance languages or into the Picard dialect, perhaps for the use of specialists such as the cathedral builders. One thirteenth-century manuscript, written in the same dialect as Villard's, is still preserved and can be consulted in the Bibliothèque Sainte-Geneviève in Paris. Its author concerned himself with mathematical problems: "If you want to find the area of an equilateral triangle. . . ." "If you want to know the area of an octagon. . . ." "If you want to find the number of houses in a circular city. . . ." The solutions to these problems are explained in detail and accompanied by supplementary figures. The spirit and style of this text are echoed by Villard:

> How to find the mid-point of a drawn circle. . . . How to measure the diameter of a column, only part of which is visible. . . . And if you wish to see a good and easily made wooden roof, study this one.

However, it cannot be supposed that Villard de Honnecourt or the other architects of his age had acquired a profound knowledge of geometry, trigonometry, or algebra. The knowledge of these cathedral builders must have been above all empirical. Yet it is quite likely that contact with this science helped to give more mathematical accuracy to the development of the plans and elevations of the great cathedrals.

Two designs on page 39 in the *Sketchbook* * showing a group of squares merit particular attention. Under the center one in the plan is written: "How to lay out a cloister with its galleries and courtyard." However, there is no further explanation and this design needs commentary. The exterior square is twice the size of the inner one and is obtained by tracing the diagonal of the smaller square and then constructing a square having this diagonal as one of its sides. This new square is twice as large as its predecessor. In other words, the first square has been doubled and the result drawn around it. The cloister garden has an area equal to half that of the whole cloister; the scale or ratio is 2 : 1, an ele-

* Bowie, *op, cit.*, plate 55.

Villard de Honnecourt's "Sketchbook": detail of page 39

mentary proportion frequently found in medieval construction. Medieval designers clearly showed a preference
for simple relationships (2 : 1 and 1 : 2, 3 : 1 and 1 : 3).

Units of measure varied from one city to another, and
architects avoided scaling their plans and were particularly interested in proportions which could be transposed
from plans to actual scale or dimension without having
to use a scale. In the *Sketchbook* under the rectangle
placed almost directly below the squares of the cloister
is this explication: "How to divide a stone so that each
of its halves is square." This must not be taken too
literally because in practice stones are never cut this way.
In this square * the diagonals connecting the sides to
the middle have been drawn. The inner square thus
obtained is one-half the area of the former.

The interest in these two designs on page 39 at first
does not seem justified and there is nothing truly remarkable about them at all. For Villard or "Master II," the
supposed continuer of the *Sketchbook,* these two designs
do not seem to have been any more important than the
twenty or so other designs on the same page. But what
is interesting is that these two rectangles caught our
attention when we were leafing through an extraordinary
document published in Regensburg more than two centuries later, in 1486(?), by the German architect Mathias
Roriczer with the permission of the bishop of that city.
The work is modestly entitled *On the Ordination of*

* *Ibid.,* plate 55-J.

123

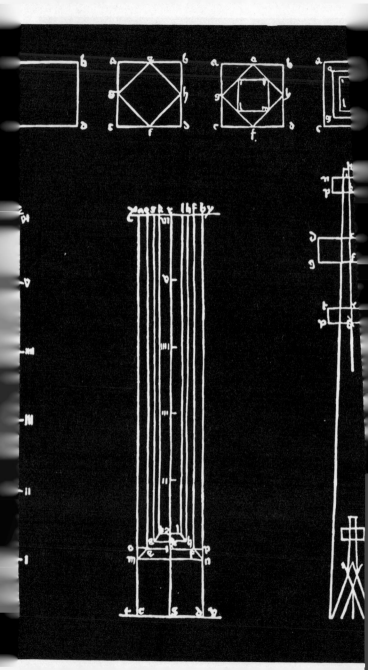

Pinnacles. We were immediately struck by the resemblance between Roriczer's designs and those on page 39 of Villard's *Sketchbook.* The German's designs are much more detailed and explicit as well as more difficult to understand for those unaccustomed to reading documents on geometry and unfamiliar with problems of construction. Roriczer explains how to design correctly a pinnacle based on a plan. He constructed one square inside another following the method employed by Villard, and in this inner square he constructed a third one; he then rectified these squares so that they fit one within another like the rectangle on page 39 of the *Sketchbook.** From this the pinnacle grew little by little. The real interest in this operation is that Roriczer is actually in the process of revealing the secret of the masons. The masons' secret according to this architect would therefore be the art of taking an elevation from a plan. This method of designing pinnacles is in actuality a general method of designing also the other parts of a cathedral, whence its importance.

A document from 1459 confirms Roriczer's statement. In that year master masons from such cities as Strasbourg, Vienna, and Salzburg met at Regensburg in order to codify their lodge statutes. Among other decisions, they decided that nothing was to be revealed concerning the art of taking an elevation from a plan to those who were not in the guild: "Therefore no worker, no master, no 'wage earner,' or no journeyman will divulge to anyone who is not of our guild and who has never worked as a mason how to take the elevation from the plan."

These two documents, Roriczer's and that of the assembly of 1459, have often led historians to premature conclusions about the secret or secrets of the masons. What was a secret in the fifteenth century was not necessarily one in the thirteenth. Professional organization had profoundly changed during the twelfth and thirteenth centuries. Attention has been called to the dividing-line marked by the end of the thirteenth century in medieval history and the history of construction. Beginning at that time, architects came to organize themselves on the basis of the guild system and came to agree,

* *Ibid.*, plate 55-O.

125

Plan and elevation of a pinnacle according to Roriczer

little by little, not to communicate to outsiders the technical and scientific knowledge they had acquired through exchanges with the outside world during the ascendant period of the Middle Ages.

Plate 39 of the *Sketchbook* proves that Villard de Honnecourt knew the principle which permitted the taking of an elevation from a plan, but the thirteenth-century architect did not consider it to be a secret. Moreover, the professors who taught geometry – then one of the seven liberal arts – and art itself in the universities taught their students Plato's method of doubling a square. The solution is found in *Meno*, in a dialogue between Socrates and a slave. This Platonic passage is therefore indirectly related to the origin of the method used to take an elevation from a plan and the secret of fifteenth-century stonecutters. About two thousand years separate Plato and Roriczer. Remembering this, it is fascinating and moving to listen to the discourse between Socrates and the slave:

SOCRATES (to the slave): Tell me, my friend, do you know that this space is square?

Socrates is reported to have traced, on the ground or elsewhere, the figures necessary to his demonstration.

SLAVE: Yes.

SOCRATES: And that in a square space, the four lines that are there are equal?

SLAVE: Without doubt.

SOCRATES: And that these lines which cross the middle are also equal?

SLAVE: Yes.

SOCRATES: Can a space of this kind be both larger and smaller?

SLAVE: Certainly.

SOCRATES: If one gives to this side two feet and to the other two equal feet, what will be the overall dimension? Examine the thing like this: if it has, on this side, two feet, and, on this side, only one, is it not true that the space would have one times two feet?

SLAVE: Yes.

SOCRATES: But from the moment that the second side has two feet, that makes it two times two feet, doesn't it?

SLAVE: Yes.

SOCRATES: How much are two times two feet? Figure it out and tell me.

SLAVE: Four, Socrates.

SOCRATES: Could one not have another space twice the size of this one but similar, and with all the lines equal?

SLAVE: Yes.

SOCRATES: How many feet would it have?

SLAVE: Eight.

This Platonic dialogue did not pass unnoticed by the Romans and by Vitruvius who preserved it. The cathedral builders could therefore have learned the solution of doubling the square in the university, but much more directly by reading Vitruvius' *De Architectura*. This is the text by the Augustan architect which was doubtless known to medieval stonecutters:

First of all, among the many very useful theorems of Plato, I will cite one as demonstrated by him. Suppose there is a place or a field in the form of a square and we are required to double it. This has to be effected by means of lines correctly drawn, for it will take a kind of calculation not to be made by means of mere multiplication. The following is the demonstration. A square place ten feet long and ten feet wide gives an area of one hundred feet. Now if it is required to double the square, and to make one of two hundred feet, we must ask how long will be the side of that square so as to get from this the two hundred feet corresponding to the doubling of the area. Nobody can find this by means of arithmetic. For if we take fourteen, multiplication will give one hundred and ninety-six feet; if fifteen, two hundred and twenty-five feet. Therefore, since this is inexplicable by arithmetic, let a diagonal line be drawn from angle to angle of that square of ten feet in length and width, dividing it into two triangles of equal size, each fifty feet in area.

Taking this diagonal line as the length, describe another square. Thus we shall have in the larger square four triangles of the same size and the same number of feet as the two of fifty feet each which were formed by the diagonal line in the smaller square. In this way Plato demonstrated the doubling by means of lines, as the figure appended at the bottom of the page will show. *

The design by Vitruvius is lost.

The square was not only used to determine harmonious proportions for a cloister or to design pinnacles based on a plan, but also to establish the plans of certain churches. The American archaeologist Sumner Crosby of Yale University, who conducted a series of excavations at Saint-Denis after the last war, has come to the conclusion that architect Pierre de Montreuil based the reconstruction of the nave and transepts on an *ad quadratum* or square plan. The inclusion of such a long passage from Crosby is justified by the fact that it explains with maximum clarity the ideas behind a particularly engaging problem:

An attentive study of the nave and transepts proves that the plan of Pierre de Montreuil's constructions at Saint-Denis spring from it [an *ad quadratum* plan]. The geometrical problem of how to divide a square into nine equal squares and then subdivide the four corner squares into four still smaller squares each was resolved by the simplest means. Parallel lines dividing the sides of the square into three equal parts intercept diagonals at four principal points (the crossing), giving birth to nine equal squares. Perpendiculars dividing the corner squares in two divide each into four small squares. The solution is self-determining and is based strictly on intersections of 45° and 90°. Despite a certain number of irregularities, it is evident that this system was used at Saint-Denis to locate the placement of the transept piers. These irregularities appear only at those places where the new construction had to be

---

* English transtation from Morris Hicky Morgan, *Vitruvius, Ten Books on Architecture*, Cambridge (Mass.), Harvard University Press, 1926, 252.

joined to that of the twelfth century. A module * of 325 mm. must have been used. The "royal" or "Parisian" foot measured 324.84 mm. It is quickly realized that its use permitted the construction of a square that, with only the slightest corrections, matched the twelfth-century masonry and allowed the foundations of the nave which had been projected in the twelfth century to be used in the thirteenth for the new nave walls. This was the module which determined all of Pierre de Montreuil's major dimensions: the name and transept bays are 6.50 m. long, or 20 modules, measured from the center of one pier to another; the sides of the crossing measure 13 m., or 40 modules, as does the width of the nave, with a slight increase in width to the west so that it could be set on the twelfth-century foundations. Reusing the twelfth-century foundations caused the side aisles of the nave to be 7 m. wide, a deviation from the module. Another important dimension which seems to have been calculated on the module in accord with the general proportions of the transept was the height of the nave keystones which has been called 29 m. But in point of fact, the distance from the pavement to immediately under the keystones of the ogives is 26 m. It is obviously difficult to determine with what scale the master of the works calculated the heights of the main vaults. And it must be remembered that the present level of the pavement is only approximately where it was in the thirteenth century. But, accepting the 26 m. measurement, the total is exactly 80 modules, which means that the proportion of the nave width to its height is 1 : 2. . . . The impeccable logic which resulted from the use of simple geometric principles produced harmonious proportions. **

The history of doubling the square, the Regensburg statutes, and Roriczer's book must not make one overlook the existence of the famous passage in Étienne Boileau or the Regius or Cooke manuscripts in England, all of

* A module is a variable unit of length used to serve as a basis for the planning measurements of a building.
** Sumner McKay Crosby, *The Abbey of St.-Denis, 475-1122*, New Haven, Yale University Press, 1942.

which imply the existence of masons' secrets. In effect, the seventh paragraph of the forty-eighth statute concerning masons, stonecutters, plasterers, and cementers by Boileau reads as follows: "Masons, cementers, and plasterers may have as many aides and valets in their service as they wish, as long as they show no one of them any point of their trade."

It has been very accurately noted that this forty-eighth statute is the only one of the 101 entered by Boileau that includes any mention or suggestion of a secret, which has given rise to the idea that such a text was applicable only to the trade of construction. But it is essential to point out that the paragraph in question is addressed not only to stonecutters and dressers, but to workers located right at the bottom of the guild scale: to masons, cementers, and plasterers. The guild master certainly did not ask his workers to conceal from their aides and valets techniques as complicated as those permitting the elevation of a spire to be taken from its plan for the very simple reason that these workers did not have the knowledge required to comprehend the geometrical ideas necessary to carry out such a project. More probably, the guild master demanded that his workers not reveal, for example, the proportion of the diverse elements which went into the composition of mortar and plaster or how to recognize stones of high quality. This passage refers more to tricks of the trade than to true secrets. The word "secret" does not really apply here. Moreover, this famous paragraph cannot really be understood if it is not considered with reference to the rest of the forty-eighth statute. It came about with the increasing desire of the king and the guild master to control a trade which until that time had developed freely.

The two English manuscripts mentioned above – the Regius, written about 1390, and the other, the Cooke of about 1430 – contain numerous similarities since they were adapted from the same manuscript which had been drawn up about 1360 and contained both an account of masonic practices and the legendary history of that profession. The Regius was drawn up by a cleric particularly interested in religion and in moral precepts, and the Cooke by an author very devoted to the trade. These

130

two manuscripts were not professional statutes as were those of Étienne Boileau or those of London in the fourteenth century, although they have certain points in common. Recopied through the centuries with many variations, they form what are known as the masonic *constitutions*. They are an important connection between actual masonry and honorary freemasonry. The customs or practices are divided into two parts: the "Articles" which are addressed to masters, and the "Points" which are addressed to workers. The latter must love God and the Holy Church, accept money humbly, not fight among themselves and, finally, conduct themselves discreetly. The following is the appeal for discretion contained in the Cooke manuscript:

> "The third point is that he [the worker] keep secret the counsels of his fellows, whether given in the lodge, in the chamber, or any other place where masons be."

And from the Regius, a more precise limitation:

> The third point must be stressed with the apprentice, therefore know it well. He keeps and guards his master's teachings and those of his fellows. He tells no man what he learns in the privacy of his chamber, nor does he reveal anything which he sees or hears in the lodge or anything which happens there.
>
> Disclose to no man, no matter where you go, the discussions held in the hall or in the dormitory; keep them well, for your greater honor, lest in being free with them you bring reproach upon yourself and great shame upon your profession.

Masonic historians have for a long time thought that secrets which workers were ordered not to reveal were of an esoteric nature, but this has no basis, and we agree with Knoop and Jones who have written on the matter:

> It is well known that there were "secrets" because the Articles and Points forbid their revelation; but there is no reason to suppose that these secrets contained anything more esoteric than the remarks or discussions in the lodge (which did not need to be told to employees) as well as technical secrets of the trade

concerning, for example, the design of an arch or the manner of placing a stone so that as much of its grain as possible followed the position it had had in the quarry bed.

This chapter cannot be closed on the subject of the "secret" without a word about the origin of the signs which today permit freemasons to recognize one another. The builders of French or English cathedrals never needed secret grips or signs to recognize a fellow builder. According to Knoop and Jones, this custom was born in Scotland where special conditions in working stone caused highly specialized workers to adopt secret means of knowing one another. In part, these conditions were due to the existence of a category of apprentices, the "entered apprentice," not found anywhere else, and to the absence of freestone in Scotland. Scottish workers capable of cutting this quality stone were faced with the impossibility of proving their skill, and constant competition from less skilled workers called *cowans* who originally built dry-stone walls. To prevent cowans from being hired for work at which they were not qualified, stonecutters decided to adopt signs of recognition known only to themselves. In a document from the Mother Kilwinning lodge in 1707 there is proof of what was done: "No mason will give work to a cowan without the password. . . ."

These signs of recognition were known to exist in sixteenth-century freemasonry and must have been carried over into Scottish honorary freemasonry as it developed in the seventeenth century. The custom was then transmitted from Scotland to England. Reciprocally, masonic constitutions went from England into Scotland, where they had been unknown originally.

Due to many archives and incised inscriptions we know the names and works of several of the great thirteenth-century cathedral builders. In a previous chapter the text of the Amiens labyrinth was cited. There are found the names of the three architects who succeeded each other from 1220 to 1288 in directing the works of that cathedral: Robert de Luzarches, Thomas de Cormont, and his son Regnault. The inscription of the Reims

erneuil-sur-Avre: tombstone of a master mason(?)

labyrinth showed that the choir begun in 1211 was the work of Jean d'Orbais; the work was continued by Jean Le Loup and Gaucher de Reims. The façade and the great rose were the work of Bernard de Soissons, who worked there about thirty-five years between 1255 and 1290. This Bernard de Soissons had a rather good income because in 1287, in a register of the tax assessments levied to pay for the coronation of Philippe le Bel, he was taxed in two parishes: in that of Saint-Denis for five sous and in that of Saint-Symphorien for one hundred sous.

Also known is the name of the very talented architect of the beautiful Church of Saint-Nicaise at Reims, now destroyed. Like a great many other architects, he had the honor of being buried in the church he had built. On his tombstone is written: "Here lies Master Hugues Libergier who began this church in the year of the Incarnation 1229 on Easter Tuesday and who died in the year of the Incarnation 1263 the Friday after Easter. Pray to God for him." This tombstone is now in the cathedral where it can be admired, and observed that Hugues Libergier, dressed in a long robe, holds the instruments of his profession: a square, a compass with crossed arms, and a graduated rule.

Notre-Dame de Paris: fragment of the inscription on the south transept

Another celebrated tombstone is that which honors in particularly remarkable terms the memory of Pierre de Montreuil, the architect who reconstructed the nave and transepts of Saint-Denis. He also built the refectory of the Abbey of Saint-Germain-des-Prés and the Lady Chapel at that same abbey, in which he was buried. This is his epitaph:

> Here lies Pierre de Montreuil, a perfect flower of good manners, in his life a doctor of stones. [O] that the King of Heaven will conduct [him] to the highest of poles!

It will be noted that he was given a "university" title: Doctor of Stones (*doctor lathomorum*).

Even after his death, Pierre de Montreuil's prestige was so great that his wife was honored by being buried in the chapel at his side. Proof also of the esteem paid to women of humble origin is contained in her epitaph: "Here lies Anne, formerly the wife of the late master Pierre de Montreuil. Pray God for her soul."

Still another epitaph praised the architect of the thirteenth-century choir of the abbey church of Saint-Étienne in Caen: "Here lies Guillaume, very elevated in the art of stones, who accomplished this new work."

But by far the most astonishing inscription is that which is cut over a distance of some twenty-five feet along the lower jambs of the south transept of Notre-Dame de Paris. It tells who created this transept: "Master Jehan de Chelles commenced this work for the glory of

the Mother of Christ on the second of the Ides of the month of February 1258." What nineteenth- or twentieth-century architect has been honored by having his name inscribed in such a remarkable manner on a building he has built?

It ought to be noted that all these inscriptions date from the second or last third of the thirteenth century. By that time the architect was fully aware of his worth, and the thirteenth century probably witnessed a change in the architect's status: an architect no longer participated manually in the operation of the workshop. Indeed, he diverted work from himself. The words of Nicolas de Biard in the middle of the century testify to this change. This preacher was enraged to see men of "a mechanical art" no longer doing manual labor. He wrote that in the larger workshops

> it was the custom to have a principal master who gave only oral orders, was very rarely on the job, or never used his hands, although he received a much larger salary than the others. . . . The masters of the masons, carrying a baguette and gloves, ordered others to "cut it for me there" and worked not at all, although they received a larger payment; it is this way with many modern prelates.

The word *magister,* which precedes the words *cementarius* and *lathomus,* frequently indicated an architect, although not always. The word *magister,* or "master," was, moreover, borrowed by the mechanical arts from the liberal arts. Originally, *magister* applied only to those who had completed the study of the liberal arts. In the thirteenth century Doctors of Law were moved to anger because carpenters adopted this honorary title with no right to it. *Magister operis* is very often translated as "master of the works," an expression that *sounds* very medieval but which is unhappily incorrect. This expression is not, like "architect," a word designating a professional man. One is master of the works of such and such a church or such and such a great lord. For example, one could be master of the royal masonry works. *Magister operis* can designate an architect but it

136

Strasbourg Cathedral, façade: plan "B" and the present façade (over)

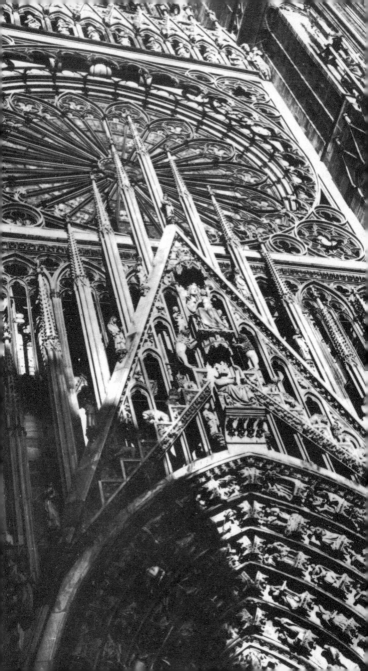

can also indicate a foreman or overseer. In England the master of the works is very often a functionary designated by the king to supervise works in progress. The architect is he who conceives the plan and draws up specifications, creative work that must have been executed in a "drafting room" that was probably reserved for the architect and his assistants.

During the whole period of the cathedral crusade architects do not seem to have made wood or plaster models. This ancient means of showing edifices seems to have survived for a time in the early Middle Ages and then disappeared for several centuries only to reappear during the Renaissance. There are unhappily very few plans left from the early Middle Ages. Villard de Honnecourt's *Sketchbook* includes elevations but they are designs executed as a basis for later works rather than original working plans. Villard drew the ground plans of three churches: the Abbey of Vaucelles, Notre-Dame of Cambrai, and Meaux Cathedral. But these are not complete, precise plans.

How can one explain the absence of documents as fundamental as plans? It must be remembered that there was no particular reason for saving plans of completed buildings; and even today it is difficult to obtain plans of important buildings erected in the early part of this century. No one has seen any reason for saving them. Also, earlier medieval plans must often have been executed on sheets of plaster or wooden planks. The high cost of parchment perhaps prohibited its use as a drawing material. It is only by chance that so many fourteenth- and fifteenth-century parchment plans are preserved, or is it rather because this material cost less then?

The best known thirteenth-century designs are the Reims Palimpsest [9] and the plans from the Strasbourg Cathedral. In 1838 original plans dating from about 1250 were found in a manuscript at Reims belonging to the cathedral chapter. The writing which covers at least half of these plans dates no later than 1270. Parchment was very expensive and it was used over and over again. One of the designs which has been read, although it is under more recent writing, shows the elevation of a large church. This design, which John Harvey believes can be attributed to Hugues Libergier or one of his collaborators, has this remarkable feature: its author, having drawn a vertical axis through the middle of the façade, drew only broad outlines on the right half while showing details on the left.

The Museum of the Fabric at Strasbourg possesses a series of very interesting designs. The first, called "A," represents the first project for the Strasbourg Cathedral and must have been executed around 1275. There is a second design, called "B," which is a copy of "A" with the addition of the decorative elements executed on the façade toward 1300.

Detailed specifications such as those drawn up in 1284 for the reconstruction of the Church of the Cordeliers [Gray Friars] at Provins served to complete plans. It has been observed that in the Middle Ages plans were only very rarely numbered. Note that in the following extract from this specification the measurements of certain elements are given in feet:

> In the name of the Father and of the Son and of the Holy Spirit. Amen. This is the specification for the Convent of the Minor Brothers of Provins. First, the convent will be razed to the ground. And the [new] front gable and the side will be of the same dimensions that they were before, so that the side of the aisle will be on round pillars and on arches of cut stone the length of the old aisle. And the voussoirs of these arches will have a height which will require a separation so as to rejoin the entablature which supports the framework of the nave [roof]; and there will be on this side as many arches as there are bays between two tie-rods as the length of the old aisle required, and these arches will be of the dimensions required by the framework. And there will be at the springing of these arches to the gable on the side of the courtyard a buttress projecting six feet and with three bonded feet which will be tied in to a beveled facing above the support for the gable.

Nicolas de Biard was right when he maintained that the "principal master" received a much larger salary

140

than the others; but he should not have been offended by it, for it is quite normal that men capable of directing a workshop, drawing plans, and establishing specifications, have a social and financial status higher than that of the masons and stonecutters.

Chapters found themselves in the position of applicants for the services of these exceptional men who embodied so many moral qualities and so much technical knowledge. The number of men who possessed this combination of qualities and knowledge was of course limited. It became

necessary to retain architects by contracts advantageous to them. Even so, it was only hoped at the same time that they could be kept from going to other workshops during the duration of their contract. Architects would not always accept this clause restricting their freedom.

Architects obviously profited from this privileged position to determine their own working conditions. The most amusing case – and also one of the most extreme – is the contract extracted from the Archbishop of Lugo by the architect Raymond in 1129. Pierre du Colombier

Saint Éloi saves the Church of Saint-Martial from fire (fourteenth century)

has observed that in his contract Master Raymond took pains to insure that in the event currency values were to drop during the course of his employment as master of the works at the cathedral, he would be paid principally in kind. To wit, he was to receive each year six silver marks, thirty-six meters of silk, seventeen loads of wood, as many shoes and gaiters as he needed, and two sous each months for his food, plus one measure of salt and one pound of candlewax.

The advantages of payment in kind were numerous. More often than not architects were housed gratis. They were given "robes," occasionally made of fur, and they could be made exempt from taxation. In addition to all these advantages, they were often given a bonus at the end of the year. They could be engaged by the year, for the duration of the workshop or, rarely, for life, in which case provision was made for breaking the contract if the master were to become an invalid.

Architects also bettered their financial situation by giving expert advice. Following the collapse of a vault, or after a fire, a chapter often decided to call together at a fixed date some of the better known architects before repairing the damage or rebuilding. These experts would carefully survey the damage and then together draw up their conclusion. The chapter, after having properly housed and fed them, paid them considerable sums compared to what architects received annually.

Thanks to beneficial contracts and these surveys, architects became rich enough to buy houses. It was noted above that Bernard de Soissons owned two houses at Reims. They bought quarries and occasionally sold stone for the work on the cathedral where they were employed. Litlle by little certain of them established themselves as contractors although apparently they could accept only the operation of small workshops. The contracts for these small projects were awarded, just as today, to the lowest bidder.

Risking their livelihood, architects became urbanists and drew up plans for new cities, adopting circular plans like that of Bram in Languedoc, or grids like that of Aigues-Mortes. Some specialized in constructing fortified châteaux, others in the construction of bridges. The legend

Maures (Cantal): a circular city

of pontifical brothers going from one city to another to build bridges is much more romantic than factual. Numerous archives relate legal transactions or agreements concerning bridge construction but none makes any mention of the pontifical brothers.

Toward the middle of the eleventh century, Abbot Pons of Aniane signed an agreement with Geffroi, Abbot of Saint-Guilhem-du-Désert, for the construction of a bridge over the Hérault. The former undertook to transport all wood, stone, lime, gravel, iron, and lead to the site and to furnish all the rope required. The latter agreed to build half the bridge at the expense of the monastery and to pay the master of the works.

At Arles on the June 15, 1178, forty-one days before the coronation of the Emperor Frederick in that city, an agreement was reached between Jean de Manduel and the people of Arles on one side and the Jews on the other. The latter were bound to a base service of one hundred years to contribute every Holy Saturday to construction. This requirement was replaced by the payment of fifty sous and an annual fine of twenty sous in the future.

What was true about the legend of the brothers of the bridge is that there actually were confraternities which were formed in different cities, independently of one another, to tax travelers and to assure the upkeep of bridges and the payment of tolls. The brothers of the Pont-Saint-Esprit, for example, disappeared only in 1794.

145

THE MONASTIC BUILDERS

The history of monastic construction is in some ways quite different from cathedral construction, especially in connection with workshops, laborers, and the choice of plans. Yet monastic construction is another important manifestation of the creative genius of the Middle Ages close to that of the primary subject of this book. Specific characteristics of the cathedral builders can be brought very sharply into focus at the same time that certain questions of organization common to all types of religious construction can be explained. Monastic archives add much unique information to our knowledge of the subject.

The detailed account that the Benedictine monk Gervase of Canterbury wrote on the reconstruction of the church choir, following the fire of 1174, is particularly moving and informative. Thanks to this single document, life in a twelfth-century monastic workshop can be relived. Immediately after the fire the monks at Canterbury took measures to have the damage repaired and called in various experts:

> French and English artificers were therefore summoned, but even these differed in opinion. On the one hand, some undertook to repair the aforesaid columns without mischief to the walls above. On the other hand, there were some who asserted that the whole church must be pulled down if the monks wished to exist in safety. This opinion, true as it was, excruciated the monks with grief, and no wonder, for how

147

could they hope that so great a work should be completed in their days by any human ingenuity. *

It is of special interest that the monks did not have in their community any "builders." They engaged a French architect, Guillaume de Sens, who, like Villard de Honnecourt a century later, was an expert in masonry and carpentry.

However, amongst the other workmen there had come a certain William of Sens, a man active and ready, and as a workman most skillful both in wood and stone. Him, therefore, they retained, on account of his lively genius and good reputation, and dismissed the others. . . . And he, residing many days with the monks and carefully surveying the burnt walls in their upper and lower parts, within and without, did yet for some time conceal what he found necessary to be done, lest the truth should kill them in their present state of pusillanimity. But he went on preparing all things that were needful for the work, either of him-

* All quotations from Gervase's account from The Reverend Robert Willis, *The Architectural History of Canterbury Cathedral*, London, Longmans & Co., W. Pickering, and G. Bell, 1845, Ch. III, 32-62.

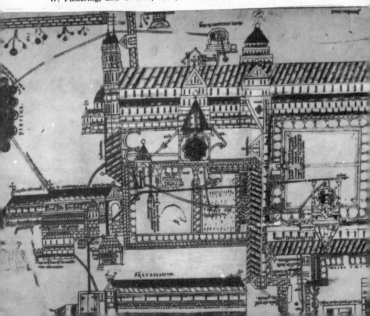

self or by the agency of others. And when he found that the monks began to be somewhat comforted, he ventured to confess that the pillars rent with the fire and all that they supported must be destroyed if the monks wished to have a safe and excellent building. At length they agreed, being convinced by reason and wishing to have the work as good as he promised, and above all things to live in security; thus they consented patiently, if not willingly, to the destruction of the choir.

Once the monks admitted the necessity of pulling down the old burned choir, Guillaume de Sens could get the stone required for the reconstruction: "He addressed himself to the procuring of stone from beyond the sea." He had a stone purchased that he knew well, that from Caen, which was one of the best available in the Middle Ages. Even today it is highly regarded across the Channel and was used in a London building project in 1955.

Awaiting the arrival of the stone, Guillaume became an engineer: "He constructed ingenious machines for loading and unloading ships, and for drawing [hoisting] cement and stone." Villard de Honnecourt was therefore not unique; the architects of the Middle Ages were all but forced to be engineers. Guillaume occupied himself at the same time in furnishing templates for the stonecutters – a work often delegated to a specialist called a "dresser," who worked with a large compass called a "dresser's compass." In fact, architects and dressers were often confused in the Middle Ages, the former represented in certain illuminated manuscripts holding one of these large compasses. According to a modern stone-cutting manual, the dresser traced working drawings, rendered on his plans vault, archivolt, and intrados templates with which he shaped his stones. They were then cut and dressed on all sides by the stonecutters under his direction.

Pierre du Colombier has added to this:

He [the dresser] even prepared the area or surface on which he outlined in large scale the face of a vault or some other piece of work with all its projections. [10]

149

While everything was being readied to rebuild the church, the old choir was pulled down, a dangerous task begun by pike-men (*piqueurs*), specialists infrequently mentioned in the texts: "The choir thus condemned to destruction was pulled down, and nothing else was done that year."

Here Gervase interrupts his narrative of life in the workshop to describe the old choir, then begins again his account of the construction year by year:

> The Master began, as I stated long ago, to prepare all things necessary for the new work, and to destroy the old. In this way the first year was taken up. In the following year, that is, after the feast of St. Bertin (Sept. 5, 1175), before the winter, he erected four pillars, that is, two on each side, and after the winter two more were placed, so that on each side were three in order, upon which and upon the exterior wall of the aisles he framed seemly arches and a vault, that is, three *claves* [bays] on each side.... With these works the second year was occupied. In the third year he placed two pillars on each side, the two extreme ones of which he decorated with marble columns placed around them, and because at that place the choir and crosses were to meet, he constituted these principal pillars.... In the summer [of the fourth year], commencing from the cross, he erected ten pillars, that is, on each side five ... and he was, at the beginning of the fifth year, in the act of preparing with machines for the turning of the great vault, when suddenly the beams broke under his feet, and he fell to the ground, stones and timbers accompanying his fall, from the height of the capitals of the upper vault, that is to say, of fifty feet.

Crippled by the fall, Guillaume was bedridden. The accident proves that in the second half of the twelfth century architects were still "on the job," working manually as the work progressed, despite Nicolas de Biard's comments. The master stayed in bed under medical care but his health did not improve:

> Nevertheless, as the winter approached, and it was

151

necessary to finish the upper vault, he gave charge of the work to a certain ingenious and industrious monk, who was the overseer of the masons; an appointment whence much envy and malice arose, because it made this young man appear more skilful than richer and more powerful ones. But the master reclining in bed commanded all things that should be done in order. And thus was completed the ciborium between the four principal pillars. In the keystone of this ciborium the choir and the crosses seem as it were to meet. Two ciboria on each side [the vaults of the eastern transept] were formed before the winter; when heavy rains stopped the work. In these operations the fourth year was occupied and the beginning of the fifth. . . . And the master, perceiving that he derived no benefit from the physicians, gave up the work, and crossing the sea, returned to his home in France. And another succeeded him in the charge of the works; William by name, English by nation, small in body, but in workmanship of many kinds acute and honest.

The technical knowledge acquired by the young monk during the several years he had been in direct contact with the work obviously was insufficient to permit him to take sole charge of the fabric after Guillaume de Sens returned to France.

Unfortunately, there were never schools of stonecutters or architects in the orders which could assure the building of monasteries without outside help.

He [William the Englishman] in the summer of the fifth year finished the cross on each side, that is, the south and the north [transepts], and turned the ciborium which is above the great Altar, which the rains of the previous year had hindered, although all was prepared. . . . Thus was the fifth year employed and the beginning of the sixth. In the beginning of the sixth year after the fire, and at the time when the works were resumed, the monks were seized with a violent longing to prepare the choir, so that they might enter it at the coming Easter. And the master, perceiving their desires, set himself manfully to work, to satisfy

the wishes of the monastery.... They [the monks] had remained in the nave of the church five years, seven months, and thirteen days. And returned into the new choir in the year of grace . 1180, in the month of April, on the nineteenth day of the month, at about the ninth hour of Easter Eve.... And thus was the sixth year employed, and a part of the seventh ... which, in short, included the completion of the new and handsome crypt, and above the crypt the exterior walls of the aisles up to their marble capitals.... In the eighth year the master erected eight interior pillars, and turned the arches and the vault.... He also raised the tower up to the bases of the highest windows under the vault. In the ninth year no work was done for want of funds.

If a monastery as rich and as powerful as Canterbury lacked funds for a whole year to pay workers and buy materials, it can easily be understood that the building of more modest monasteries, parish churches, or cathedrals might require several centuries.

153

In the tenth year the upper windows of the tower, together with the vault, were finished. . . . The tower was covered in, and many other things done this year [1184].

Thus concludes Gervase's account. With but one exception, the monks took no part in the actual reconstruction of their choir. But this is not an unusual case. In England some decades ago, G. G. Coulton questioned the active role of monks as builders, a thesis which occasioned heated debates in various large trade publications. Coulton accused Montalembert's work *Les Moines d'Occident* (written in the nineteenth century) of having been the origin of what he called the legend of the builder monks. The Coulton "school" continued this polemic for some time. Today tempers are calm and it is easier to see the truth although it must not be forgotten that this is one of the most complex problems of medieval architecture.

Apologists defending Montalembert's thesis have often turned to the early twelfth-century writer Orderic Vitalis who wrote that "all Cistercian monasteries are built in clearings in the midst of forests and the religious build them with their own hands." But this must be cited cautiously. In the first place, Vitalis cited the Cistercians, *not* the Benedictines, as being builders; and, in the second place, so far as the Cistercians were concerned, the term "the religious" included hired laborers – lay workers – as well as the brothers themselves. Any history of monastic construction is complicated by this situation which cannot be clarified unless the differences between the Benedictines and the Cistercians are listed. Then, so far as the Cistercians themselves are concerned, a distinction must be made between work done by the brothers and by hired laborers.

To understand the differences between the two orders, one must return to St. Benedict's Rule. Concerning construction it is mute, however: there is not one word about it. The mission of the monk is to consecrate his life to God through meditation, prayer, and offices. The Rule organized his life for God's work. Manual labor was encouraged only in as much as it contributed to that end,

154

and then only "regulated in consideration for the weak." Harvesting – very hard work – could be done only as an exception. The Rule encouraged such work as gardening or that carried on in workshops. The spirit of the Rule did not anticipate the hard work of the quarryman, the stonecutter, or the sculptor.

The Benedictine historian Ursmer Berlière confirmed this when he wrote that

> the monastic order, by reason of its constitution which presupposes a life of solitude, can participate only in limited measure in great agricultural or manual labors.

And he added that even this measure decreased or even disappeared with the elevation of members of the order to the priesthood (monks were not priests in St. Benedict's day).

As monasteries became economically and socially more important, farming and such manual labor as house-cleaning were entrusted to servants (*famuli, canonici, matricularii, ministerales*) who frequently made up a considerable part of a cloister's population. It was a useful and advantageous situation for freemen or serfs.

In the eleventh century reformers in southern Germany and Italy had the idea of making religious brothers out of these layman, and they came to be called *frères convers* ("converted brothers" or "working brothers"). This solution had the advantage of preventing frequent contact by monks with the outside world, a contact harmful to meditation and the spiritual life. The idea of laborers attached to the orders was revived and codified by Cîteaux, which published in 1119 the "uses and customs" of its working brothers. Henceforth, there were two categories of the religious: monks, who consecrated themselves entirely to a spiritual or intellectual life, and working brothers who did physical tasks. These latter had to take vows of poverty, chastity, and obedience, but they could never become priests or monks. They had their own refectory and dormitory, and worked as farmers, shoemakers, stonecutters, tanners, blacksmiths, and masons. Through the work done by their working brothers, the Cistercians did play a part in the construction of their monasteries, but the history of the reconstruction of Clairvaux and the stonecutters' marks found in Cistercian buildings prove nonetheless that they must have called in outside constructors.

It is not without interest to study the construction of a twentieth-century monastery to understand certain problems of the past. The Benedictines today have adopted the Cistercian practice of using *frères convers*. At the beginning of this century, the Benedictine monks of Buckfast Abbey in Devonshire, having discovered the original twelfth-century Cistercian foundations, decided to rebuild their church. The abbot had no "builder" among his working brothers so he sent a young *frère convers*, Brother Peter, to the Abbey of En Calcat in France to learn some of the fundamentals of masonry from the specialists who were rebuilding that abbey. Brother Peter returned to England at the end of eighteen months and worked in the workshop day after day for thirty-two years. Today he is seventy-six years old and his hands have been burned by lime from his often difficult work. Seeing his hands thus scarred makes it clear why workshop foremen during the Middle Ages regularly bought gloves for their masons.

Brother Peter taught the rudiments he had learned at En Calcat to four or five working brothers. They worked primarily as cementers and masons and, in exceptional cases, stonecutters, a profession requiring a very long apprenticeship. When funds were available stones were bought already cut at the quarry.

The abbot, conforming to the "uses and customs" of the working brothers, gave them dispensations from certain offices. They had only to attend the first office in the morning and Complines at night. Thus the *frères convers* were able to work without interruption from morning until night. The number of working brothers the abbot could assign to the workshop was limited by the very life of the monastery. In assigning too many of these brothers to the work, he risked disrupting the regularity of the monastic routine so indispensable to meditation and the divine service. It seemed necessary that one-third of the community be working brothers in order for a Benedictine monastery to operate smoothly.

Statistics published by the papacy in 1935 seem to confirm this ratio. Of about ten thousand Benedictines, thirty-three per cent were, or were destined to be, working brothers. The problem of recruiting these working brothers is as acute today in prosperous countries such as England as it was at the end of the thirteenth century in western Europe.

To supervise the *frères convers,* the abbot asked for a volunteer from among the monks. Father Richard, who agreed to be the "Father-constructor," is now seventy-nine years old and has paid dearly for his physical efforts during so many years. He had no dispensation from attending morning offices. Frederick Walters, a lay architect, was called in to draw the plans and give professional supervision to the works. At Buckfast Abbey there were no monks who had studied architecture before taking orders as these were in some other contemporary monasteries.

When it was known that the monks at Buckfast were beginning to rebuild their monastery, gifts flowed in which accelerated the work. The roofing and carpentry were done by specialists from the outside. Generous donors offered a gold high altar, the stations of the cross, and the choir stalls. The monks themselves were busy: while some of the fathers such as Dom John Stephen, the abbey historian, continued their intellectual studies, others, such as Dom Norris, prepared to paint the immense fresco which now decorates the ceiling of the lantern tower. The church was finished in 1936. If Dom Robert had then been a monk at Buckfast, he probably would have executed a tapestry for the church. Buckfast Abbey is now one of the most famous and most frequently visited places in England, thanks to the working brothers' construction and the monks' decoration.

The reconstruction of the monastery of Landevennec at the extreme end of Brittany, under way since 1950, clearly exposes the advantages and disadvantages of voluntary labor. The Bishop of Quimper wrote a pastoral letter bringing to the attention of his diosecans the Abbot of Kerbénéat's project to rebuild Landevennec Abbey. He invited them to welcome the fathers who passed through the parish. The parish priests exerted themselves to discuss the Benedictine project from the pulpit. They requested volunteers to help the monks dig and terrace the ground at Landevennec to make way for the reconstruction of the church and adjoining buildings. The Breton population responded with faith to this appeal, and groups of farmers could be seen leaving their homes during the winter months from December to February to participate in this good work. Parishioners with their tools left before dawn in groups of twenty to fifty in order to be on the site at Landevennec by dawn and returned to their village only at nightfall.

It is plausible that volunteers in the Middle Ages did the same thing in winter, yet it appears equally improbable that peasants could have left the fields during the harvest. This benevolent work at Landevennec was, as in the Middle Ages, essentially base labor, although it was no less important for this reason. Indeed, this aid was particularly appreciated at Landevennec because it came at a time when the monks had scarcely sufficient funds to offer laborers *any* part. It has been estimated that nearly twelve hundred working days were put in by these volunteers.

Along with this appeal for volunteer labor, the abbot organized, with the cooperation of the cities and towns in the Diocese of Quimper, a great charity fair in which the population actively participated. With the funds thus obtained the monks were able to engage a constructor from Landerneau for the actual construction of the abbey. In 1958, scarcely eight years after the first call for help, the brothers of Kerbénéat were able to reoccupy the venerable site of Landevennec, through the active help of the people of Brittany.

Proven methods used to realize Le Corbusier's plans

Chapelle Notre-Dame du Haut - Ronchamp

Financement de la Construction

PARTICIPATION DE 100 Fr.

Série 3   Nᵒ 007279

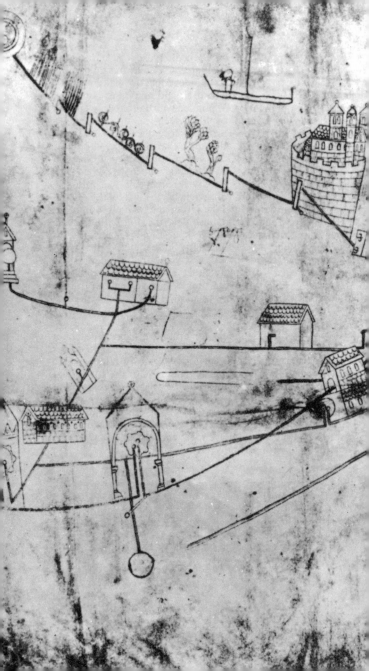

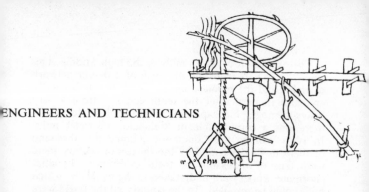

ENGINEERS AND TECHNICIANS

The history of technology proves that the cathedral builders were active participants in Europe's first industrial revolution. The history of technology is a recent study, and few historians are as yet involved with the fascinating problems it raises. This history is different from that of the sciences, which have been very much studied. Unhappily, the history of science is of more limited interest for a knowledge of the past, for few societies have been scientific although all, without exception, have been technical.

The degree of a nation's inventiveness seems bound up with certain laws. The pattern develops much faster when a society is growing, when that society is intellectually stimulated and founding its ideals. The pattern slows down when the society, having reached maturity and prosperity, fears changes which could bring with them new technology.

Natural sources of power are, today as yesterday, the basis of a nation's industrial power. The three principal sources of power during the ascendant period of the Middle Ages were water, wind, and the horse. Their importance cannot be overestimated. Economic life today would come to a halt without gasoline; without water power, the life of the Middle Ages is unthinkable.

The water mill was known in Asia Minor in the first century B.C., but it was not fully exploited then because of climatic and hydrological conditions in the Mediterranean basis, the true center of ancient civilization. The mills at Barbegal in Provence, operated at great expense, are an example of the great difficulty the Roman world had in utilizing water power.

161

The expansion of water mills in the high Middle Ages stemmed in part from the presence of a denser network of rivers and the regular, annual floods in the far north, and also in part, after the tenth century, from a very heavy demographic expansion. During this later epoch there was a considerable multiplication of water mills. In 1086 William the Conqueror counted five thousand of them in England, and by the thirteenth century there were tens of thousands of them in France. In cities enormous works were undertaken to dig canals by which mills could be installed. In the country all the rivers were regulated. Water power was advantageous because it was available everywhere. In Toulouse, city engineers succeeded, despite the rapid, often violent current and rising water, in throwing a great embankment nine hundred feet long against the river, diverting its course diagonally to create a waterfall powerful enough to operate the mills at Bazacle. To finance the construction of this causeway and for the upkeep of such a titanic work, a great sum of money had to be collected. The city's businessmen set up a company on shares. Each stockholder then shared in the losses and gains prorated according to his investment.

The introduction of water mills into the system of seignorial rights brought forth a ban on manually operated mills.

Thanks to the intervention of the cam shaft, rotary movement was transformed into reciprocal movement, and thus hydraulic power could not only grind grain, but could be used to card wool, make beer, reduce oak bark to powder for tanning, forge iron, and make paper.

It seems inconceivable that the word "artisan" was used to designate the men who built and operated those machines which in large measure replaced manual labor. It sufficed then, as now, to have a clutch to disengage moving gears. If we decide to continue using the word "artisan" for the Middle Ages, we will certainly have to resign ourselves to the fact that in the year 2500, when automation reigns supreme, our industry – of which we are so proud – will be considered just as artisan-like.

From the twelfth century on innumerable windmills were built to profit from the inexhaustible Aeolian energy.

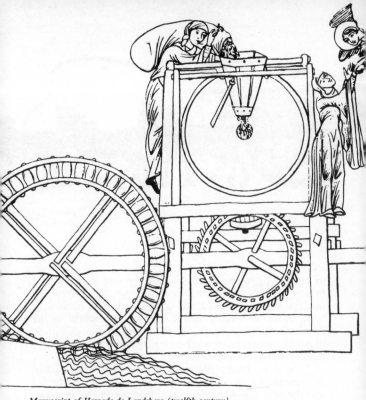

Manuscript of Herrade de Landsberg (twelfth century)

Even mills activated by the sea-tide were built. The Middle Ages preceded the electricity of France in this domain.

The horse was a source of considerable power for the Middle Ages. Cathedral workshops profited directly from it. Maximum capacity of the horse was achieved for the first time in the history of the world. This better use was due to the combined use of a series of inventions. To protect its feet, it was shod; the large-stone roads of the Romans were replaced by more yielding paving. Harnesses were changed: the girth, which had been placed at the horse's throat, was modified to become a shoulder collar which permitted a more efficient use of the animal's strength, a system which, moreover, had the advantage

163

of permitting horses to be hitched together in teams one behind another. Oxen which were slow and difficult to manage were then frequently abandoned. The horse thus contributed to a rapid rise in the Western world in the development of uncultivated land, and in the execution of much construction work by bringing building material right to the foot of the project.

Paralleling the development of these sources of power, all human activities progressed. Weaving was perfected and the spinning-wheel invented. Iron was made stronger; wheels were made to turn easier; the mechanical pendulum was invented. Experimental agriculture was practiced; artesian wells were dug; crop production increased; vineyards were improved. Compasses and post-rudders were adopted. Chimneys were built and coal burned; wax candles provided light. The fork was conceived; glasses were worn; the mirror appeared. Paper was made.

Their writings testify that the men of this epoch were conscious of the advantages of technics. The author of a Cistercian report observed that the disciplined use of the forces of nature frees the laborer from the burdensome mechanical labor that a machine could do. The Franciscan monk Bartholomew understood the importance of iron not only for war but also for agriculture and construction. In 1260 he wrote:

164

From numerous points of view iron is more useful to man than gold, even though the covetous desire gold more than iron. Without iron man could not defend himself against his enemies or enforce communal law; the righteous assure their [enemies'] defeat by means of iron, and the dishonesty of the wicked is punished with iron. Also, all manual labor demands the use of iron without which land cannot be cultivated or houses built.

This technical achievement was possible only because medieval society believed in progress and did not cling to outmoded traditions. It could and did improve its conditions. Said Gilbert de Tournai:

Never will we find truth if we content ourselves with what is already known. . . . Those things which have been written before us are not laws but guides. The truth is open to all, for it is not yet totally possessed.

Emile Bréhier, in his *Philosophie du Moyen-Age*, wrote that this freedom regarding authority, which at least manifests itself in the precise and rational choice of a thesis, is joined to a belief in the possibility of progress which without doubt made itself clear for the first time in the Middle Ages. John of Salisbury, having cited Abélard's statement that a modern man was capable of composing a dialectic which owed nothing to the ancients, added to this what Bernard (Master of the episcopal school at Chartres from 1114 to 1119) had said:

We are as dwarfs mounted on the shoulders of giants, so that although we perceive many more things than they, it is not because our vision is more piercing or our stature higher, but because we are carried and elevated higher thanks to their gigantic size.

The cathedral builders, working in a society that recognized progress, were inventive, and the cathedral at the end of the thirteenth century was the result of hundreds of innovations and more or less important perfections due to the constructors' spirit of research.

Most of the trades developed simultaneously, and often

the progress of some helped the development of others. For example, progress by the blacksmiths aided architects, sculptors, and stonecutters. Indeed, blacksmiths were cathedral builders in that they made stronger steel tools to cut harder stone, such as that of Volvic, near Clermont, which until then had resisted man. Also, after this, sculptors were able to carve more delicate images from stone. The use of the harder stones meant that architects could design thinner walls and columns of a smaller diameter.

Tools, being harder, required less sharpening. A blacksmith's equipment consisted of a forge, an assistant, an ax-case, a laborer charged with collecting tools to be sharpened and returning them, and a laborer charged with feeding the forge coal and wood. Unhappily, little is known about the origin and the social situation of these blacksmiths, who must have formed a group separate from other builders. There was a forge at the workshop and in each of the quarries being used. At Autun about ten per cent of the expenditures were expenses of the forge: "To the forge of Autun, for the year, 42 livres 10 sous 6 deniers. . . . To the forge at the quarry, 3 livres 2 sous."

Blacksmiths not only forged tools, slings (straps of iron for lifting large stones), nails of all types, horseshoes, tie-rods (such as those used at Westminster Abbey to prevent its walls from spreading), but also iron chains which architects imbedded within the masonry of a wall as reinforcement.

The architect of Saint-Chapelle put chains through its walls. Experience has shown that this means of reinforcing a building is not the best since it causes ruptures in the masonry. Here we find ourselves faced with an evolution in technique which finally proved not to be progress. Today architects frequently use new methods of construction and new materials rashly, but do they always know their quality? There will doubtless be many surprises.

The Franciscan cited above had good reason to underline the importance of iron in the construction of his time. Thanks to the blacksmiths, carpenters had at their disposal perfected tools which permitted the improvement of carpentry, shoring, and scaffolding.

The technique of sawing timber had not been lost during the high Middle Ages although the technique of stonecutting had practically disappeared. Carpenters had to adapt centering to the evolution of the vault. Thirteenth-century centering constructed for the ogival vaults of the great cathedrals was a true marvel, the result of multiple perfections.

Carpenters knew how to adapt their skills to the particular conditions of their locality or time – to the absence of large beams, for example. Villard de Honnecourt concerned himself with this problem, and explains how to construct a tower, a house, or a bridge with small timber: "How to work on a house or tower even if the timbers are too short." "How to make a bridge over water, with twenty-foot timbers." In the twelfth century it was already difficult to find large trees because the forests had been devastated. Suger recounts with his usual verve how, despite the contrary advice of specialists, he discovered in the forest of Iveline, "thanks to God and the Holy Martyrs," some trees of a very large diameter, essential to the reconstruction of Saint-Denis:

When the work had been finished in great part, when the stories of the old and new building had been joined, and when we had laid aside the anxiety we had long felt because of those gaping cracks in the old walls, we undertook with new confidence to repair the damages in the great capitals and in the bases that supported the columns. But when we inquired both of our own carpenters and those of Paris where we might find beams, we were told, as was in their opinion true, that such could in no wise be found in these regions owing to the lack of woods; they would inevitably have to be brought hither from the district of Auxerre. All concurred with this view and we were much distressed by this because of the magnitude of the task and the long delay of the work; but on a certain night, when I had returned from celebrating Matins, I began to think in bed that I myself should go through all the forests of these parts, look around everywhere and alleviate those delays and troubles if [beams] could be found here. Quickly disposing of other duties and hurrying in the early morning, we hastened with our carpenters, and with the measurements of the beams, to the forest called Iveline. When we traversed our possession in the Valley of Chevreuse we summoned through our servants the keepers of our own forests as well as men who knew about the other woods, and questioned them under oath whether we could find there, no matter with how much trouble, any timbers of that measure. At this they smiled, or rather would have laughed at us if they had dared; they wondered whether we were quite ignorant of the fact that nothing of the kind could be found in the entire region, especially since Milon, the Castellan of Chevreuse (our vassal, who holds of us one half of the forest in addition to another fief) had left nothing unimpaired or untouched that could be used for building palisades and bulwarks while he was long subjected to wars both by our Lord the King and Amaury de Montfort. We however – scorning whatever they might say – began, with the courage of our faith as it were, to search through the woods; and toward the first hour we found one timber adequate

168

to the measure. Why say more? By the ninth hour or sooner we had, through the thickets, the depths of the forests and the dense, thorny tangles, marked down twelve timbers (for so many were necessary) to the astonishment of all, especially those on the spot; and when they had been carried to the sacred basilica, we had them placed, with exultation, upon the ceiling of the new structure, to the praise and glory of our Lord Jesus, Who protecting them from the hands of plunderers, had reserved them for himself and the Holy Martyrs as He wished to do. Thus in this matter Divine generosity, which has chosen to limit and grant all things *according to weight and measure,* manifested itself as neither excessive nor defective; for not one more [timber] than was needed could be found. *

Medieval carpenters were very skilful in shoring up constructions, whether by means of underpinning or by modification of the first floors, and they could intelligently adapt their scaffolding to the particular conditions

* English translation from Panofsky. *op. cit.*

The Life of Saint Alban *(about 1250)*

of a given building. In order to construct the circular keep at Coucy, which had a diameter of about 102 feet, they had the ingenious idea of attaching a very slightly inclined spiral ramp to the wall. Wagonloads of material could be drawn up along this ramp without difficulty.

Thirteenth-century miniatures show the wheelbarrow, an astonishingly small apparatus, made by carpenters so one man could do the work of two. Yet the wheelbarrow is still used extensively in building skyscrapers in the United States. For a long time attributed to Pascal, this invention was perhaps the fruit of the imagination of a simple carpenter of the cathedral crusade.

Roofers, working in direct collaboration with carpenters, were persons of equal importance. One of them, Master Pierre of Dijon, was housed at Autun in 1294 in a house built at the expense of the fabric. If carpenters had to adapt themselves strictly according to the evolution of vaults, roofers had to adapt themselves to changes in supports. In antiquity there was rarely any need to roof large buildings; but the Middle Ages, developing in northerly countries, frequently had to develop covering to protect buildings from rain and snow. Depending on the region, churches were covered with tile, lead, or slate. Roman tiles were replaced by large flat tiles and the lead roofing already employed in the high Middle Ages was so well planned that it was always possible to remove a defective piece and easily replace it. Solid and durable tiles covered churches in the west and north of France by the end of the twelfth century.

Roofers knew how to decorate the coverings of their churches beautifully. Lead was decorated with paintings appliqued on the metal by means of very active mordants. Roofers made two-tone mosaics, profiting from the fact that slate has different reflective values depending on the side used.

The care and importance attached to the roof are eloquently proved by the considerable sum (5000 livres) that Maurice de Sully bequeathed to the cathedral to cover the superstructure of the choir of Notre-Dame de Paris with lead. To protect their edifices against rain, architects realized a network of little trenches. They invented the gargoyle, a water spout to direct jets of water away

from the walls. To facilitate maintenance of their work, they created service passages at different levels on the building and perfected spiral stairways. These passages and stairs permitted circulation in case of fire. It is well known that architects began building their churches in stone to diminish the risk of fire. To vault these edifices they adopted methods known from antiquity, Byzantium, or the Orient: broken barrel vaults, cupolas on pendentives or squinches, or groined vaults. They perfected them to cover larger and larger expanses. In particular, they had the idea of reinforcing simple groined vaults with ogives (ribs) that seem to have strengthened the vault at its weakest points, that is, along the web joints and at the crown. The ogival, or rib vault, which architects know to have an amazing plasticity, was a technical advance, but it is now known that it did not have the primordial importance so long attributed to it. The construction of this type of vault, which was generalized by the mid-twelfth century, was made possible by skilled stonecutters, a better choice of materials, and the use of a more solid mortar.

The flying buttress, a revolutionary invention of the twelfth century, not only efficiently counter-buttressed the ogival vaults, permitting naves to rise higher and higher, but it saved numerous older vaults which had threatened to collapse.

In opening larger and larger windows to light church interiors, architects elevated glassmakers to the first rank of cathedral builders. Thanks to the monk Theophilus, we probably know glassmaking best of all medieval crafts. He introduces himself to us in this manner:

I, Theophilus, an humble priest, servant of the servants of God, unworthy of the name and profession of a monk, to all wishing to overcome or avoid sloth of the mind or wandering of the soul, by useful manual occupation and delightful contemplation of novelties, send recompense of heavenly price. . . .

Where is the author of a technical tract today who would preface his work with so much humility and faith? Theophilus continues:

172

When you shall have reread this often, and have committed it to your tenacious memory, you shall thus recompense me for this care of instruction, that as often as you shall successfully have made use of my work, you pray for me for the pity of Omnipotent God, who knows that I have written these things, which are here arranged, neither through love of human approbation, nor through desire of temporal reward, nor have I stolen anything precious or rare through envious jealousy, nor have I kept back anything reserved for myself alone; but in augmentation of the honour and glory of His Name, I have consulted the progress and hastened to aid the necessities of many men. *

These moving passages by the monk Theophilus help us understand better the spirit with which the cathedral builders worked. If a certain consception of progress, a fruitful, inventive spirit, and particularly favorable economic and social conditions were all necessary to the construction of cathedrals, to make possible such miracles of stone as Notre-Dame de Paris or Notre-Dame de Chartres, other conditions of a spiritual order were equally essential; but, as was indicated above it is impossible to cover here this aspect of the subject. To be complete, such a study would require research far beyond our competence. But this discretion obviously must not be interpreted as a negation or depreciation of the spiritual role. The cathedrals testify to inspired wisdom as much as to ingenious science; it is brought to us through the pictures in this book.

* Theophilus, *An Essay upon Various Arts . . . Forming an Encyclopedia of Christian Art of the Eleventh Century*, trans. by Robert Hendrie, London, John Murray, 1847, xlvi and li of the preface.

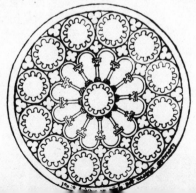

THE END OF A WORLD

The creative genius of the cathedral builders expired at the end of the thirteenth century. The enthusiasm of the people for the cathedral crusade waned considerably. The desire to set records which had so passionately raised naves and spires ever higher toward heaven no longer inspired constructors. In fact, the maximum possibility in this domain seems to have been reached: the choir vaults of Beauvais Cathedral, which were the world's tallest, collapsed in 1284. Vivid colors gave way to more subdued shades. Stained glass windows tended to disappear.

The faith which had been at the base of the cathedral crusade was no longer so lively. The religious fervor which had so marvelously propelled the growing Middle Ages and which had made that time one of the greatest periods in human history lost its intensity. Roger Bacon, author of an astonishing teaching reform that could have rejuvenated medieval Christianity, was thrown into prison. The freedom of expression that had been honored in the universities became suspect. Canon law clashed with Roman law, which legislators called up from the past. Nationalism made its appearance and papal authority and prestige decreased. The great monastic orders founded no new abbeys and could recruit working brothers only with difficulty.

Eloquent proof of this religous crisis, particularly significant by reason of the circumstances of its issuance, is provided by Bishop Guillaume le Maire of Angers, who had been requested by Pope Clement V to make a

175

report on the religious situation in France for the Council of Vienne in 1311. He painted a dramatic picture of the situation:

In many places in the kingdom of France there has been established an irreligious custom or, rather, an abominable abuse. In effect, it occurs that on Sundays and other important holy days dedicated to the Majesty of Heaven, when Christians ought to abstain from all mercenary works in order to go to church to spend their time at the divine office and to receive the word of God, of which they have so great need, from prelates and others having the right to preach – these days are chosen for holding fairs, law hearings, and councils. It even happens that the faithful, having more of a taste for things of the flesh than of the spirit, leave the church and its offices to meet in such places where they practice their business or their legal affairs. So it follows that on these holy days when God ought to be adored above all, it is the Devil who is adored; the churches remain empty; the courts of justice, taverns, and workshops resound with quarrels, tumult, and blasphemy; perjuries and crimes of nearly every kind are perpetrated. It follows that the Law of God, the articles of faith, and all other things pertaining to the Christian religion and to the salvation of the soul are almost totally ignored by the faithful. God is blasphemed, the Devil is revered. Souls waste away, the Catholic Faith is wounded.

It is interesting to realize that this document came from a man who had also called attention to himself in demanding suppression of the Order of Templars. The decadence of the "holy army" praised by St. Bernard was a symptom of the exhaustion of Christianity's greatest possibilities. The condemnation of the Templars, although obtained by iniquitous means and for selfish motives, was at the same time the consequence of a certain weakening of the order itself and the shattering sign of the end of a world.

Parallel to this halt of religious zeal and creative thought, technical progress and economic expansion both

176

came to a standstill. All the great medieval inventions came before the end of the thirteenth century. For nearly 150 years nothing new was invented; only existing inventions were perfected, except in the military world the cannon was created in the fourteenth century. The magnificent prosperity of the thirteenth century was approaching its end. Society began to grow rigid and sclerotic. The middle class that emerged from the first industrial revolution in Europe, during which faith and civic pride had contributed to the financing of cathedrals and hospitals, formed dynasties at the end of the thirteenth century and desired the social status quo. They stinted their donations to the cathedral chapters. Com-

"God is blasphemed, the Devil is revered..."

munes bankrupted themselves and lost their liberty to the expanding royal centralization. Free work and free competition, responsible for the growing European economy, disappeared to the profit of organized guilds or corporations which one might say were "patrons exploiting a monopoly." Sons succeeded fathers and those who reached responsible positions were not necessarily the best qualified or most skillful.

No new cities were founded; land clearing came to a halt and colonization leveled off.

Inflation increased dangerously and nothing could stop it. In the course of the Middle Ages there had always been devaluations; but it appears that the one effected by Philippe le Bel at the beginning of the fourteenth century was particularly resented. A charming song of 1313 recalls is:

> *Il se peut que le roy nous enchante*
> *Premier nous fit vingt de soixante*
> *Puis de vingt, quatre, et dix de trente*
> *. . . Or et argent tout est perdu,*
> *Ne jamès n'en sera rendu* *

* It seems that the king enchants us
For at first sixty made twenty for us,
Then from twenty, four and from thirty, ten
. . . Gold and silver, all is lost,
None of it ever to be returned.

The earliest representation of a cannon (1326)

The beginning of the economic crisis which struck Europe was announced by the resounding crash of the great Italian bank of the Scali in 1337.

The Hundred Years' War began that very year, bringing with it more ruin and misery. Gradually most of the workshops in France were abandoned, and churches left unfinished. Workshops for war replaced workshops of the Faith, building fortresses and fortifications. No longer was there free circulation from one region to another, and stone from a particular quarry could not be hauled long distances. Local stone was used and a knowledge of different quarries vanished.

The population of builders was decimated by epidemics and fighting. Those who survived were nearly all impressed into war service. There they lost their love of and skill in delicate craftsmanship – fortified castles required nothing more than rough work. The sculptors of Chartres and Reims cut crude blocks or even made cannonballs; in these desolate times there was no longer a place for sculpture. And when the horrible war ended more than a century later, only a handful of builders was left in France. They tried to organize themselves into companies, but these professional organizations remained isolated from each other.

By contrast, German builders, not involved in the Hundred Years' War and its devastations, had continued to work in the great cathedral shops and succeeded, in the security of relative peace, in establishing ties between the corporations or stonecutters' lodges of far distant . regions. In 1459 the master stonecutters met at Regensburg to unify the statutes of different lodges. Thus there existed in Germany a vast organization of builders in the middle of the fifteenth century. It seems that this organization had then reached its apex. Before the end of that century the architect Roriczer had already broken from this association by publicly revealing a technique that the Regensburg assembly had recommended be kept secret. In the sixteenth century the organization was to be in danger, but until their disappearance in the seventeenth and eighteenth centuries, lodges in Germany remained the meeting places of craftsmen.

In England and Scotland the evolution of lodges was

Workshop accident (fourteenth century)

12h

136

Grimnus

different. Professional lodges tended to become honorary. After the fourteenth century, but especially in the sixteenth and seventeenth centuries, English and Scottish masons came to accept men who were not builders but who were interested in the former's craft for different reasons and who attended their meetings and formed part of their membership. This led to the distinction between working measons and fraternal masons. The earliest honorary or fraternal masons who joined these professional lodges were doubtless clerics ordered by the king, lords, or ecclesiastics to supervise workshops. The author of the famous Regius manuscript was such a man. Then sheriffs or city mayors joined them. Cultured men interested in geometry could join these lodges to study the knowledge of architects on the subject – geometry was one of the seven liberal arts and as such merited study and respect. Ardent men of letters, antiquarians, sometimes joined these lodges, perhaps to study ancient architecture, perhaps hoping to have access to the knowledge and secrets of the past. The Regius and Cooke manuscripts, or variations of them which were read in the lodges, seemed to justify the antiquarians' interest in the masons' trade, since these manuscripts had the cathedral builders descended from those of very early antiquity, in particular the builders of Solomon's Temple. Knoop and Jones have very brilliantly analyzed the written sources from which imaginative authors took these legends that frequently came directly from Biblical or medieval readings.

Little by little the ratio of laborers to cultivated men in these lodges diminished, and the history of the English cathedral builders may be considered terminated with the formation of the Great Lodge of London in 1717. From then on honorary freemasonry continued to prosper, and it has been very justly defined by Knoop and Jones as being a "particular system of ethics clouded by allegories and illustrated by symbols."

The end of the cathedral builders in France was less spectacular. In the course of the sixteenth century they became masonry contractors for Renaissance architects.

At the end of the Hundred Years' War, chapters undertook – with an admirable faith – to try to inspire the handful of builders who had preserved the old traditions as well as the whole population to a new cathedral crusade. And for a century, until the wars of religion, canons obstinately persisted in trying to complete abandoned cathedrals despite multiple material and spiritual difficulties. They were worthy successors to the great canons of the twelfth and thirteenth centuries; yet they seem not to have been conscious that the world around them had profoundly changed, that the builders were no longer those of the great epoch, that the people no longer had the faith which had motivated men during the rise of Christianity.

The spirit of initiative and inventiveness that had made great the builders of the Middle Ages no longer existed; these men repeated almost mechanically, without faith or inspiration, the works of earlier times. They were not in touch with their own times and they were congealed in the techniques and forms of a lost time. They were capable only of varying the decoration of stones on a skeleton that had been perfected two centuries earlier.

Corporatively organized, builders fought ceaselessly to defend their rights and privileges, restraining the pious enthusiasm of the canons. Jealous of their prerogatives, some builders would not hesitate to have recourse to the law courts when their rights were challenged. Some seem to have spent more time in court than at the shop. And no longer did the most qualified accede to the title of "master." The laborer no longer held any hope of becoming a master because in the corporation sons succeeded fathers, nephews succeeded uncles. Chapters could complain that these worthless nepotists were debauched, drunken idlers, but they were forced to hire them. To strengthen themselves, corporations limited entrance to "mastership," and different chapters were consequently led to dispute bitterly for the services of one architect.

If the canons were disgusted by the "builders," they were even more greatly deceived by the people's indifference to the House of God. The profound and exalting faith of the twelfth and thirteenth centuries, which had brought the cathedrals soaring from the earth, no longer elevated souls or enflamed hearts. Despite the foundation of new religious confraternities to collect funds, despite papal appeals and indulgences accorded to benefactors, despite episcopal generosity and royal subsidies, the combined sums were never sufficient to finish the work. The people, without whom nothing great can ever be accomplished, no longer responded to appeals on behalf of the cathedrals. A contemporary report stated with sadness and resignation that the great undertakings of earlier times were no longer possible, *charity having been extinguished*.

General History	*Architectural History*
1031 Accession of Henri I	ca. 1030-1080 Abbey of Conques
	1031 Sainte-Marie of Ripoll consecrated
1054 The Greek Schism	1045-1080 Saint-Hilaire at Poitiers
1057 Charter of the franchise of Orléans	ca. 1050-1150 Le Puy Cathedral
	1062-1083 Abbey of the Trinity at Caen
	1063 San Miniato at Florence consecrated
	1065 St. Mary at Cologne consecrated
a. 1065 *Chanson de Roland*	ca. 1072-1092 Lincoln Cathedral
1066 Norman conquest of England	
1074 Reformatory decrees by Gregory VII	
1077 Meeting at Canossa	
1077 Commune of Cambrai	
1078 Turkish invasion of Asia Minor	1078-1128 Cathedral of St. James at Compostella
1085 Toledo falls to Islam	ca. 1080-1108 Abbey of Saint-Benoît-sur-Loire
1094 Valencia captured by the Cid Campeador	1088-1109 Abbey of Cluny
	1093-1130 Durham Cathedral
1095 Urban II preaches the First Crusade at Clermont	1095-1500 Cathedral of San Marco at Venice
	ca. 1096-1132 Abbey of Vézelay

1098	Foundation of the Cistercian order	1100	Moissac Cloister
1099	Jerusalem captured by the Crusaders	1101-1128	Angoulême Cathedral
1108	Accession of Louis VI		

		1120-1178	Saint-Front at Périgueux
1112	St. Bernard enters Cîteaux	1120-1178	Autun Cathedral
1118	Foundation of the Templars		

1122	Suger becomes abbot of Saint-Denis	1130-1147	Abbey of Fontenay
1122	Peter the Venerable becomes abbot of Cluny	ca. 1130-1147	Tournai Cathedral
1126	School of Translators at Toledo	ca. 1133	Sens Cathedral
		1137	Narthex of Saint Denis
		ca. 1145	South tower at Chartres
		ca. 1151	Noyon Cathedral
1136	Abélard teaching in Paris	ca. 1153	Senlis Cathedral
1137	Accession of Louis VII	ca. 1160	Laon Cathedral
1138	Beginning of rivalry between Guelphs and Gibelines	ca. 1160	Cistercian Abbey of Pontigny
1145	St. Bernard preaches the Second Crusade	1163	Cathedral, Notre Dame de Paris
1152	Eleanor of Aquitaine divorces Louis VII	1175	Canterbury Cathedral
1153	Death of St. Bernard	ca. 1194	Bourges Cathedral
		1194	Chartres Cathedral

1170	Martyrdom of St. Thomas Becket	1211	Reims Cathedral
1180	Accession of Philip Augustus		
1187	Saladin recaptures Jerusalem		
1189	The Third Crusade		

1204 The Fourth Crusade - Capture of Constantinople

1209 Beginning of the Crusade against the Albigensians

1214 Battle of Bouvines
1215 Official birth of the University of Paris
1215 Approbation of Minor Friars (Franciscans)

1216 Foundation of the Order of Preaching Friars (Dominicans)

1221 Death of St. Dominic
1226 Death of St. Francis
1226 Accession of St. Louis (Louis IX)

1241 The Mongols reach Central Europe

1248 St. Louis' First Crusade

1252 St. Thomas teaching in Paris

1261 End of the Latin empire in Constantinople

1265 Marco Polo's voyage to Asia (until 1295)
1268 Étienne Boileau's *Guild Statutes*
1270 St. Louis' Second Crusade. He dies in Tunis

1277 Condemnation of Thomism and Averroism
1282 The Sicilian Vespers

1285 Accession of Phillippe IV, le Bel
1291 Surrender of St. Jean d'Acre
ca. 1292 Death of Roger Bacon

1220 Amiens Cathedral
1220 Collegial of Sainte-Gudule at Brussels

1227 Trèves Cathedral
1227 Toledo Cathedral
1228 Church of St. Francis at Assisi
1229 Church of the Jacobins at Toulouse
1239 Nave of Saint-Denis
1243 Sainte-Chapelle at Paris
1245 Westminster Abbey
1247 Beauvais Cathedral
1248 Cologne Cathedral
1250 Strasbourg Cathedral
1250 Upsala Cathedral
1250 Siena Cathedral

1262 Collegial of Saint-Urban at Troyes

1273 Limoges Cathedral
1275 Regensburg Cathedral
1277 Rodez Cathedral

1282 Albi Cathedral
1284 Choir vaults of Beauvais Cathedral collapse

BIBLIOGRAPHY

[Note: Paperback editions are indicated by (P).]

I. MEDIEVAL LIFE

Coulton, G. G. *Life in the Middle Ages*, 4 vols. New York, 1931.
Haskins, C. H. *The Renaissance of the Twelfth Century*. New York, 1957. (P)
Haskins, C. H. *The Rise of Universities*. Ithaca, 1957. (P)
Huizinga, J. *The Waning of the Middle Ages*. Harmondsworth, 1955, New York, 1956. (P)
King, A. A. *Cîteaux and her Elder Daughters*. London, 1954.
Le Goff, J. *Les Intellectuels au Moyen-Age*. Paris, 1957.
Luddy, A. J. *Life and Teachings of St. Bernard*. Dublin, 1937.
Maritain, J. *Art et scholastique*. Paris, 1927.
Pernoud, R. *Lumière du Moyen-Age*. Paris, 1944.
Pirenne, H. *Economic and Social History of Medieval Europe*. New York, 1937. (P)
Pirenne, H. *Medieval Cities*. Garden City, 1956. (P)
Power, E. *Medieval People*. Garden City, 1955. (P)
Ross, J. B. and McLaughlin, M. M., eds. *The Portable Medieval Reader*. New York, 1949. (P)

II. MEDIEVAL ARCHITECTURE

Adams, H. *Mont-Saint-Michel and Chartres*. Garden City, 1959. (P)
Aubert, M. *L'architecture cistercienne en France*. Paris, 1947.
Bowie, T. *The Sketchbook of Villard de Honnecourt*. Bloomington, 1959. (P)
Cali, F. and others, eds. *Architecture of Truth*. London, 1957.
Conant, J. K. *Carolingian and Romanesque Architecture* (*Pelican History of Art* Series). Harmondsworth, 1959.
Crosby, S. McK. *The Abbey of St.-Denis, 475-1122*. New Haven, 1942.
Evans, J. *Art in Medieval France, 987-1498*. London, 1948.
Harvey, J. *The Gothic World, 1100-1600*. London, 1950.

Mâle, E. *The Gothic Image. Religious Art in France of the Thirteenth Century.* New York, 1958. (P)

Panofsky, E. *Abbot Suger on the Abbey Church of St.-Denis and Its Art Treasures.* Princeton, 1946.

Panofsky, E. *Gothic Architecture and Scholasticism.* New York, 1957. (P)

Pevsner, N. "The Term 'Architect' in the Middle Ages," *Speculum*, XVII, 1942.

Pillement, G. *Cloistres et Abbeys de France.* Paris, 1950.

Porter, A. K. *Medieval Architecture: Its Origins and Development*, 2 vols. New. York, 1909.

Seymour, C., Jr. *Notre-Dame of Noyon in the Twelfth Century.* New Haven, 1939.

von Simson, O. *The Gothic Cathedral (Bollingen Series XLVIII).* New York, 1956.

Temko, A. *Notre-Dame of Paris.* New York, 1955.

Thibout, M. *Églises gothiques en France.* Paris, 1957.

Thompson, A. "Cathedral Builders of the Middle Ages," *History*, X, 1925.

Viollet-le-Duc, E. *Discourses on Architecture.* 2 vols. New York, 1959.

Webb, G. *Architecture in Britain: The Middle Ages (Pelican History of Art* Series). Harmondsworth, 1955.

III. MEDIEVAL MASONS, CONSTRUCTION, AND ARCHITECTURAL FINANCE

du Colombier, P. *Les chantiers des Cathédrales.* Paris, 1953.

Coulton, G. G. *Medieval Faith and Symbolism* (Part I of *Art and the Reformation*). New York, 1958. (P)

Coulton, G. G. *The Fate of Medieval Art in the Renaissance and Reformation* (Part II of *Art and the Reformation*). New York, 1958. (P)

Frankl, P. "The Secrets of the Medieval Masons," *The Art Bulletin*, XXVII, 1945.

Gille, B., ed. *Histoire générale des techniques.* Partie médiévale. Paris, 1959.

Knoop, D. and Jones, G. P. *The Genesis of Freemasonry*, Manchester, 1949.

Knoop, D. and Jones, G. P. *The Medieval Mason.* Manchester, 1933.

Knoop, Jones, and Hamer, D. *The Two Earliest Masonic Mss.* Manchester, 1938.

de Lespinasse, R. and Bonnardot, F. *Le Livre des Metiers d'Etienne Boileau.* Paris, 1879.

Mortet, V. and Deschamps, P. *Recueil de textes relatifs à l'histoire de l'architecture et à la condition des architectes en France au Moyen-Age. XIe-XIIe siècle.* Paris, 1911. *XIIe-XIIIe siècle.* Paris, 1929.

Salzman, L. F. *Building in England down to 1450.* Oxford, 1952.

NOTES

1 Perhaps the best example is the façade of Saint-Vulfran at Abbeville (Somme).

2 The vaults of Beauvais Cathedral fell in 1284. While this was not the only medieval monument known to collapse, it was the most famous example and the only one rebuilt with twice as many piers as in the original building for additional strength.

3 Some indication of St. Bernard's influence on the Virgin's popularity in twelfth-century France is contained in Millard Meiss' "Light as Form and Symbol in some Fifteenth Century Paintings," *The Art Bulletin*, XXVII, 1945, 175-181.

4 Ecclesiastically, the most important cathedral in the Ile-de-France in the twelfth century was that at Sens, dedicated to St. Stephen (Saint-Étienne). Paris, Chartres, Auxerre, Meaux, Orléans, Nevers, and Troyes were all suffragans to it.

5 This "crown" is a geographical accident. Paris was neither architecturally nor ecclesiastically the center of France in the early thirteenth century. Gothic architecture did not begin in Paris.

6 Etymologically, "cathedral" is derived from the Latin *cathedra* meaning "chair." Bishops made official pronouncements *ex cathedra*. The church building in which the *cathedra* stayed became the cathedral.

7 In the Middle Ages every person was under the jurisdiction of a specific parish whose church he was required to attend and to whose support he was required to contribute. He could not change parishes without permission. Generally, the public attended services in the cathedral only on important feast days, such as Christmas or Easter. By no means was the cathedral open to the public every day. In later times, when the public came and went as it pleased and could enter the cathedral at will, the chapter erected choir screens to keep the sanctuary closed. For example, the choir screen at Chartres dates from the sixteenth century.

8 Unfortunately, the *Sketchbook* now contains only the plan of Cambrai. The elevations and other details which Villard mentions have been lost.

9 On this unique document, see Robert Branner, "Drawings from a Thirteenth-Century Architect's Shop: The Reims Palimpsest," *Journal of the Society of Architectural Historians*, XV, 1958, 9-19.

10 In others words, the dresser calculated the curvature of the arch and included it in his drawing. He also drew a "view" that showed the profiles of the bibs, voussoirs, etc.

ACKNOWLEDGMENTS

Bibliothèque nationale (Éd. du Seuil): pp. 7, 20, 67, 68, 109, 110, 113, 117, 118, 123, 124, 178. Bibliothèque Sainte-Geneviève: p. 79. Archives photographiques: pp. 10, 11, 17, 27, 33, 39, 59, 141, 146, 153. Courtauld Institute: pp. 36, 41, 54, 55, 61, 73, 148, 164, 179, 185-186, 187, 189. British Museum: p. 56. Musée des arts et traditions populaires (M. Maget): p. 166. Medieval Art (W. R. Lethaby): p. 88. Gimpel: pp. 81d, 99, 132, 135. Giraudon: p. 90. Roger Viollet: p. 102. Léon Violet: p. 96. Toulgouat: p. 70. Br. I. Birkosb: p. 155. Ina Bandy: pp. 81b, 137. Bulloz: pp. 142-143. Houvet: pp. 43, 48. Boudot Lamotte: pp. 13, 24, 150, 174. Lucien Hervé: pp. 9, 14, 19, 29, 121, 138, 171, 177. Bovis: p. 52. Glassberg: p. 4. Marker: p. 105. Étab. J Richard: p. 145.

The photo on page 92 is taken from the book *La Franc-maçon-nerie dans la Mayenne* by Marius Lepage and André Bouton.

The drawings at the beginning of each chapter are taken from the *Sketchbook* of Villard de Honnecourt (Bibliothèque nationale).

Quotations reprinted from *Abbot Suger, On the Abbey Church of St. Denis and its Art Treasures*, Erwin Panofsky, 1946, by permission of Princeton University Press; from *The Sketchbook of Villard de Honnecourt*, Theodore Bowie, 1959, reprinted with permission of distributor, Wittenborn and Company, 1018 Madison Ave., New York 21, N.Y.; from *Vitruvius. Ten Books on Architecture*, Morris Hicky Morgan, 1926, by kind permission of Harvard University Press; from *Art and the Reformation, Part II: The Fate of Medieval Art in the Renaissance and Reformation*, G. G. Coulton, 1958, by permission of Cambridge University Press; from *The Abbey of St.-Denis, 475-1122*, Summer McKay Crosby, 1942, by permission of Yale University Press. *The Two Earliest Masonic Mss.*, ed. by Knoop, Jones, and Hamer, and *The Medieval Mason*, ed. by Knoop and Jones, by permission of Manchester University Press.

The translator wishes to thank Professor Robert Branner of the Department of Fine Arts and Archaeology of Columbia University for his generous help with various aspects of the translation.